# AN INTRODUCTION TO THESE COUNTRIES IN AFRICA,
# AFRICA WORLD BOOKS COMMUNITY EDUCATION 2019

*Compiled by*
Elizabeth Gardiner

## TO WHOM IT MAY CONCERN

This document directs where any financial benefit from the sale of this book, "An Introduction to these Countries in Africa", 2019, are to be allocated.

Any revenue raised will be donated to Africa World Books Community Education and its CEO, Peter Lual Deng. This is intended to last in perpetuity.

Elizabeth Gardiner
*August, 2021*

ISBN 978-0-6486541-3-1
© Elizabeth Gardiner, 2020

Published by Africa World Books Pty. Ltd.
(www.africaworldbooks.com)

All rights reserved. No part of this publication may be reproduced, stored in a retrieval system, or transmitted, in any form, or by any means, electronic, mechanical, photocopying, recording or otherwise, without the prior permission of the publishers.

This book is sold subject to the conditions that it shall not, by way of trade or otherwise, be lent, re-sold, hired out or otherwise circulated without the publisher's prior consent in any form of binding or cover other than in which it is published and without a similar condition including the condition being imposed on the subsequent purchaser.

Design and typesetting: Africa World Books

# Africa World Books Community Education

Africa World Books Community Education (AWBCE), is a not-for-profit arm of Africa World Books. Africa World Books is a publishing Company and a book selling business which began its work in 2013. We write these books to help general readers understand that the whole process of leaving one's country, travelling to a new country and settling is a long process. It is difficult, confusing, sometimes nearly impossible to understand. We do this because we know that our relatives and friends need extra information about life in Australia and to be understood by others.

Former refugees from their own birth countries, these new Australians, can gain understanding and comfort from the programs AWBCE offers. Being a refugee brings new positive experiences, new information, as well as its own challenges and difficulties.

Another reason for preparing these Booklets, is to offer service providers knowledge to help them understand the background of experiences lived through by the former refugees.

Gaining a broad understanding of each of the Horn of Africa countries we hope will benefit service provider's work with people from six countries – Djibouti, Eritrea, Ethiopia, Somalia, South Sudan and Sudan. South Sudan is not always attributed to the Horn of Africa, but we have included it here because it borders some of the other countries and the former refugees arrived in Australia at much the same time as refugees from the other Horn of Africa countries. Plus, there is a large number of South Sudanese Australians, the estimation is around 30,000.

We will provide some short historical information, some knowledge about tribes, some mentions of religion and some understanding of traditional daily life. We talk about family relationships and how families behave in their traditional social groupings. We talk about how war, drought, floods, politics and famines drove some of its citizens away from their homeland.

We hope that this information will assist teachers, social workers, professionals – doctors, nurses, hospitals, lawyers, council workers, business-people, ordinary Australians: many of the people who will provide services for former refugees. We encourage you to do your own study to learn more: there is a great deal more to learn about each country, so these Booklets are simple, easy to understand but not exhaustive.

Africa World Books Community Education, working for the communities!

# Contents

## Djibouti

| | |
|---|---|
| Map of Djibouti with the Red Sea | 3 |
| Nomadic women | 4 |
| Social interactions in Australia | 5 |
| Religion | 6 |
| Religion and Health | 7 |
| Christian and Muslim families | 8 |
| Christians, Muslims and the Elderly | 8 |
| Communication of diagnoses/prognosis in a medical situation | 9 |
| Music | 10 |
| Locals | 10 |
| Art and Archaeology | 11 |
| Education systems in Djibouti | 11 |
| Symbols of Social Stratification | 13 |
| Healthcare in Djibouti | 13 |
| Recommended vaccinations for travelers | 14 |
| Information for Service Providers | 15 |
| Current crisis | 16 |
| Numbers | 16 |
| References | 16 |

## Eritrea

| | |
|---|---|
| Map of Africa | 18 |
| Where is Eritrea | 19 |
| Recent history in Eritrea | 20 |
| History | 21 |
| UN Sanctions | 22 |
| The Diaspora | 23 |
| General information | 24 |
| Early History | 24 |
| Colonization: Italy 1880–1941 | 24 |

| | |
|---|---|
| Great Britain's Role | 25 |
| UN decides Eritrea's fate | 26 |
| Liberation struggle 1961 – 1991 | 26 |
| The Birth of a Nation | 27 |
| President | 27 |
| Ongoing fighting and Challenges | 28 |
| Religions | 29 |
| Religion and Health Issues | 30 |
| Christians and Muslim Families | 31 |
| Christians, Muslims and the Elderly | 31 |
| Communication of diagnoses/prognosis in a medical situation | 32 |
| Role and acceptable behaviours of health professionals | 33 |
| Attitudes to pain relief | 33 |
| Information Provision | 33 |
| Settlement issues | 34 |
| Nutrition for women | 35 |
| Women | 35 |
| Cuisine | 36 |
| References | 37 |

# Ethiopia

| | |
|---|---|
| Map of Ethiopia | 40 |
| Prehistory | 41 |
| Antiquity | 42 |
| Middle Ages | 43 |
| Major Challenges | 45 |
| The United Nations | 46 |
| National Identity and Pride | 47 |
| Greetings | 48 |
| Family and Housing | 48 |
| Religion and Health Issues | 49 |
| Christian and Muslim Families | 50 |
| Christians, Muslims and the Elderly | 50 |
| Communication of diagnosis/prognosis in a medical situation | 51 |

| | |
|---|---|
| Government areas of responsibility | 52 |
|   Health in Ethiopia | 52 |
|   Education | 53 |
| Infrastructure | 54 |
| Settlement Issues in Ethiopia | 54 |
| Migration History | 55 |
| Ethiopian Australians | 55 |
| Settlement in Australia | 56 |
| References | 57 |

# Oramia

| | |
|---|---|
| Map of Oramia | 60 |
| Population | 62 |
| Economy | 62 |
| Political Groups | 62 |
| Gadaa | 64 |
| The Oromo People in Australia | 65 |
| Community Life | 66 |
| References | 67 |

# Somalia

| | |
|---|---|
| Map of Somalia | 71 |
| Political History | 73 |
| Brief History | 74 |
| 2019, 23rd October | 74 |
| Religion | 75 |
| Religion and Health Issues | 75 |
| Christians and Muslim families | 76 |
| Christians, Muslims and the Elderly | 77 |
| Communication of diagnoses/prognosis in a medical situation | 77 |
| Role and behaviours of Health Professionals and Volunteers | 78 |
| Ethnic Groups | 79 |

| | |
|---|---|
| Life Expectancy | 79 |
| Major infectious diseases | 80 |
| Somalian families and Traditions, Somalian Clans | 80 |
| General Information | 81 |
| Traditional Family Structure | 82 |
| Settlement issues in Australia | 83 |
|     Housing | 83 |
|     Money Issues | 83 |
|     Changing Family Roles | 83 |
|     Family Separation | 84 |
|     Intergenerational conflict | 84 |
|     Racism | 84 |
|     Emotional wellbeing | 84 |
|     Physical disability | 85 |
|     Literacy and language | 85 |
| Nutrition for women | 85 |
| References | 86 |

# South Sudan

| | |
|---|---|
| Map of South Sudan | 89 |
| The South Sudanese family in South Sudan | 89 |
| The Role of Cows | 91 |
| Contemporary Families in Australia and South Sudan | 93 |
| Modern South Sudanese families in Australia | 95 |
| Refugees from South Sudan and the United Nations role | 97 |
| Family Issues and Challenges | 99 |
| Legal Issues | 102 |
| Cultural | 103 |
| Education Issues | 104 |
| Health Issues | 105 |
| Nutrition | 106 |
| Children and Youths | 107 |
| Areas of Conflict | 108 |
| The Future | 108 |
| References | 109 |

# Sudan

| | |
|---|---|
| Map of Sudan | 113 |
| Sudan and Wars | 113 |
| Britain and Sudan | 114 |
| Map showing boundaries and South Sudan | 116 |
| Khartuom | 117 |
| Industries | 118 |
| War and Border Disputes | 118 |
| Demographics | 122 |
| Religion | 123 |
| Religion and Health Issues | 125 |
| Christian and Muslim families | 126 |
| Christians, Muslims and the Elderly | 126 |
| Communication of diagnoses/prognosis in a medical situation | 127 |
| Music | 127 |
| Photography | 128 |
| Education | 128 |
| Health and Population | 129 |
| Water Politics | 129 |
| The United States of America | 129 |
| Role and Behaviour of Health Professionals | 131 |
| References | 131 |

# Djibouti

*A map of Djibouti showing its place on a Map of Africa, it is situated on the northern border with the Red Sea*

Djibouti is a small, multi-ethnic country situated at the top of the Horn of Africa. It is an ancient land and has suffered from many wars over the years. Currently it is managed by one party system and a President who is in charge of all aspects of the country.

It shares borders with Eritrea, Ethiopia, Somaliland. It covers 9,000 square miles. It has 8 mountain ranges and the second lowest place on the global map. It is a key refueling and transshipment centre. It is the main port for the landlocked Ethiopian goods.

Djibouti has a population of over 884,017 people. It has the smallest number of citizens in Africa. 94% are Sunni Muslims, and have been Muslim for 1000 years. 3% are Christian of the Orthodox religion.

Djibouti is located on the Red Sea and Indian Ocean.

Djibouti City is located 21 Kms northwest of the Somali border. It is a sea port with the only sheltered harbor on the western side of the Gulf of Tadjoura.

The culture is diverse, due to the nation's Red Sea location at a cross roads of trade and commerce. The different groups are: Afars, the Issa Somalis, and they share the Muslim religion. It is a mixture of Arabian, French, Italian and Ethiopian cultures.

## Nomadic women

About a quarter of the population is nomadic, living in small huts that can be moved quickly. Currently there are terrible floods in key areas. "Nine people have died in floods in Djibouti City, capital of Djibouti, after almost a year's worth of rain fell in 2 days. The Government of Djibouti has declared a state of emergency. The News and information agency Agence Djiboutienne d'Information (ADI) said that 140 mm of rain fell in 48 hours to 21 November, 2019".

In 1862, the French started colonizing Djibouti. The Afars, originally from Ethiopia and the Issas from Somalia signed a treaty with France. The French were given land on the north coast of Djibouti.

It was 1945 when French Somaliland became a French territory. Tensions rose between the two indigenous tribes and the French, causing violence between the groups.

The French withdrew in 1977, when they established a local ruler, Hassan Aptidon. The French Army remained.

Dlibouti also was affected by all the civil unrest in bordering countries. In 1991, there was an armed uprising. This lasted two years and the government with some French help was restored. There are more women than men in the Army – 221,411 women and 170,386 men. They are aged 16 years to 49 years.

The USA have a military base, there is also a Chinese base and a Japanese military base. These put a lot of money into the country's coffers.

The latest threat was an attempted coup in 2000. Since then, there has been peace.

## Social Interactions in Australia

It is important to say that since 94% of the population are Muslims, there are certain cultural and social norms to observe. The most significant is to offer patients at a clinic or hospital a doctor or nurse of the same gender. It is wise to ask if the person has any special needs concerning how they need to be treated, such as religion. The use of an Interpreter is a must if there are any doubts about information not being understood. A professional Interpreter is better, usually, than a relative or friend or child, because the Interpreter will give the whole information and use correct terminology.

Muslim attitudes to Religion and Health, and old age has a wide range of attitudes, responses and experiences with disability: Factors such as level of education, access to medical information, and rural or urban upbringing are important.

**The Relative Status of Women and Men**. By custom and law men have more rights and higher status than women. Traditional Afar and Issa culture as well as Islam tend to support a pattern of gender roles that give men predominance in public life, business, and politics. Economic necessity, conflict, and migration have made many women the sole household head.

This fact plays a large role in how the families settle, as in Australia, where men and women are equals under the law. Many women have arrived as single parents, which is a very unusual state in Djibouti itself. Women have to bear all responsibility in this case and find the responsibilities quite challenging at first.

# Religion

Arabs were the first settlers in the country dating back in 3BC and in 825BC the religion of Islam was introduced. The French occupation of the country in the 1800s up to the late 1900s introduced Christianity to the country, but Islam still remained the religion practiced by the majority of the Djibouti people.

94% of the population practice Islam. The Somali Issas (60% of the population) and the Afars (35% of the population) are Muslims. Only 6% of the population practice Christianity. A little over 9,000 people are Roman Catholics and they are under 1 diocese. "Other Christian churches include the Protestants, the Greek Orthodox Church, and the Ethiopian Orthodox Christian (religion practiced by the Ethiopians in the country). Baha'i Faith is also practiced by a small minority. However dominant, Islam is not the state religion and there are no constraints as to what religion each person should practice. Each religion is respectful of the other". (Spain exchange, 2019).

Religious festivals are very much observed in the country. Islam and Christian festivals are celebrated as national holidays in the country. Some of these festivals include the Eid Al Adha and Eid Al Fitr for the Muslims, and Christmas and New Year for the Christians. During these religious festivals, especially for the Muslims, people wear traditional clothing as a sign of sincerely celebrating the festivity.

When it comes to the deceased, all bodies are buried, whatever religion he/she practices. There is no cremation in Djibouti. The Afars and Issas believe, however, that the souls of their dead rejoin their ancestors. (Spain exchange 2019)

# Religion and health issues

From: www.islam-usa.com/e40.html

- Cleanliness is considered "half of the faith". Qur'an, the holy book, prohibits eating pork or pork products, meat of dead animals, blood and all intoxicants.

- Respect a Muslim's modesty and privacy. Some health examinations can be done over a gown. Provide same sex health care persons, if possible. Always examine a female patient in the presence of another female.
- Some Muslim men will not shake a woman's hand.
- Provide Muslim or Kosher meals.
- Allow them to pray, and if they can read, to read the Qur'an.
- Take time to explain medical tests, procedures and treatment.
- During a birthing, it is preferred that the father be the sole male present.

There is also a range of deep cultural beliefs and attitudes in Muslim communities towards disability that need to be discussed. They are:

- A social stigma with corresponding fear of "visibility" in the community.
- A curse or punishment for some wrongdoing. This belief is evident among other cultures, such as north Sudanese.
- A gift from God or God-given, when a disadvantaged child or person is seen as a blessing.

## Christian and Muslim families

Family is the foundation of Djiboutian society. The peace and security offered by a stable family unit is greatly valued and is seen as essential for the spiritual growth of its members. A harmonious social order is created by the existence of extended families. Children are treasured, and rarely leave home until they marry.

## Christians, Muslims and the Elderly

In Djibouti there are no old peoples' homes. The practice of caring for one's elderly relatives is considered an honour and blessing, and an opportunity for great spiritual growth. God asks that we pray for our parents, but act with limitless compassion, remembering that when we were helpless little children, they preferred to help us rather than themselves.

Mothers are particularly respected in both religions. The Prophet Mohammed said "Paradise lies at the feet of mothers".

When they reach old age, Djiboutian parents are treated mercifully, with kindness and selflessness. Serving one's parents is a duty second only to prayer, and it is their right to expect it. It is considered despicable to express any irritation, if an old person becomes difficult.

Respite care and nursing homes may be used. Hospitals are also acceptable to many, however people without English are frightened about remaining in mainstream institutions.

# Communication of Diagnosis/prognosis in a Medical Situation

News of an illness is first given to the family – the closest member to the patient. The next of kin will advise the immediate family, but perhaps advice will not be given to friends.

Patients are often not told about a life-threatening disease, as it is felt that to do so might make their condition worse. They also may be ostracized by their community because people may consider them infectious and/or cursed.

Every family is different. Plus, after being in a western country for several years, the understanding of English could be fairly good, so it might be possible to tell the person gently about the diagnosis. If a patient wants to know, tell him/her.

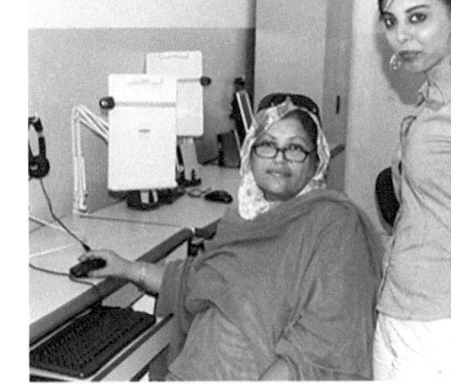

In some cases, the family leaves all the telling to the medical staff, in other families, the wisest person will manage the telling.

Words like "dying" and "cancer" are used with sensitivity, as for any group. Cancer is sometimes referred to as "That Disease". Avoid discussing death, dying and how long a person is likely to live.

When a person is dying, family and friends are called in to stay until the person passes away. The Qur'an is recited until they pass away. Once the person has died, the house is open, and condolences are received. There are no celebrations or frivolities. Burial and religious rites are performed within 24 hours.

## Music

Music is very important to Djiboutis. Afar music is like the music of Ethiopia. Afar music is shaped by Arabic influences. Somali folk law plays a big role and they used a 5 pitch scale in an octave for songs. European music has 8 notes in an octave.

The different ethnic communities residing in Djibouti each have their distinct styles of music and dances. Some of the common instruments used to play music include the oud (pear-shaped, lute-like string instrument), the tanbura (a string instrument) and drums. (world atlas. Dec. 6, 2018).

## Clothing

Locals wear European, western clothing, especially the men – jeans and a t-shirt. They also wear a cloth "skirt" along the same lines as South Sea Islanders from Tonga. Women wear a dirac, a long dress made of polyester and cotton which suits the climate.

Married women's clothing is similar to the Saris of India. Single women usually don't wear a hijab.

## Art and Architecture

There is not much emphasis on Art in Djibouti. The architecture however is varied, with French colonial buildings and Muslim mosques. Roads in the capital are sealed, with wide streets and elegant buildings. On every roof there are satellite dishes, showing that people are aware of life around the world.

## Education System in Djibouti

The education system in Djibouti was originally developed to meet a limited demand for education; it was essentially designed for elites and borrowed heavily from the French system (administrative structure and pedagogical methods). This system was not adapted to the country's realities. (Wikipedia, 2019)

About 70% of the total population and 85% of women are not literate. There are also large inequalities in access to education in regions, gender, and income levels. Moreover, the education system in Djibouti is very costly due to high unit costs for school construction, learning and teaching materials, and teacher salaries.

**Primary Education.** This takes 5 years and many more boys than girls gain an education. In the picture below, some women learn to read.

**Middle Education.** Middle education takes a further 4 years and completes the compulsory years of schooling. Traditional subjects are provided to the one quarter females and three quarters male.

**Secondary Education.**
The three years of secondary school complete the options for young people. One quarter schools are private and have a much higher standard of teaching than government schools.

**Vocational Education.**
Technical education lasts for 3 years and students receive Diplomas. There is a choice – students can do three academic years or choose to do 2 years with the third being hands-on work experience.

Djibouti has a literacy rate of 57%, life expectancy at birth is 49 years, and 26% of children under five years old are chronically malnourished. This data underscores the need to invest in human capital to alleviate poverty in Djibouti.

**Tertiary education** is studied at Djibouti's only University. It has a very high standard of teaching, due to the many visiting teachers from overseas. There are undergraduate and graduate courses. Faculties include pure science, life sciences, engineering and liberal arts.

The government of Djibouti recognizes education as essential for growth and human development. As a result, the government has placed education at the center of its development policies. In 2000, an education reform was initiated with the goal of improving access, quality, and relevance.

In 2018, rural population was 213,101, a 0.98% increase from 2017. 1960 the population was 50,000 and has grown every year since then. Rural people make up 47.38% of the population.

## Symbols of Social Stratification

In line with the socio-economic differentiation into a developing urban society and a largely stagnant agro-pastoral rural society, differences in appearance and life style between social groups are increasingly visible. The urban elites speak French, are well-dressed, have good housing, drive their own cars, and travel abroad frequently for business, education, or leisure. The rural and urban poor have substandard housing, no means of transport, and live under precarious conditions. Most of the rural populations speak Afar or Issa-Somali, not the more prestigious French.

Tourists may purchase leopard skins and rugs at a market in Djibouti City.

## Health Care

Health care in Djibouti is varied: Djibouti City has good facilities with well-trained doctors and nurses, but outside the capital health care is patchy at best. Medicine and even sterile dressings and intravenous fluids might need to be purchased from a local pharmacy by patients or their relatives.

The HIV/AIDS in Djibouti prevalence was 1.6% of the population for those aged 15–49 years old, as of 2015.[2] As of 2015, there were approximately 9,400 people living with HIV/AIDS in the country.[3] There were an estimated 600 deaths from AIDS in 2015.[3]

There were 1,007 cases of malaria in 1994. Between the mid-1970s and the mid-1990s, 23 percent of children under five were underweight. That number has risen to 29.8% in 2012.[3] In Djibouti, 93.1% females had female genital mutilation as of 2006.[2] Female genital mutilation is a leading cause of infant and maternal mortality, and it continues to be prevalent to this day, despite a 1995 law prohibiting the practice.

## Recommended Vaccinations for travelers and other Health issues

The World Health Organization recommends that all travelers be covered for diphtheria, tetanus, measles, mumps, rubella and polio, as well as for hepatitis B, regardless of their destination in the country. The consequences of these diseases can be severe, and outbreaks of them do occur.

In Australia, women and men are becoming overweight, as a result of a lack of exercise, plus some take away foods. Children have a growing problem with their teeth rotting. This needs community education. It is important to encourage people to maintain their traditional diet, while adopting healthy foods from the host country, Australia.

The issue of mental illness is one which Djiboutians have recognized in Australia. It affects older people and women are said by Muslim faith to be more susceptible to this kind of illness. Community education is needed, so that the actual numbers become known, its causes discussed and some solutions investigated.

Women who live in Australia would like to be trained in Australian law, and know their rights. Women would like training in their own language, as this better helps understanding. Their main religion is Islam and the women would like workers to understand how this impacts their lives in such a powerful manner.

## Information for Service Providers

People from Djibouti would like all service providers to know about their culture. Then their work will improve to this group, because of understanding. Please refer to the Somali Booklet for further information about Islamic cultures.

Parent(s) want to learn about their rights, the children learn from one another or online to know what their rights are. It would help single mothers to undergo some training about Parenting of African families in Australia. Despite differences in culture and religion, African families share historical differences too.

Older women and men need to spend longer in English classes, to learn how to communicate in English. This is very difficult because so many of the refugees are illiterate, especially the women. Not being able to speak, understand or read English truly holds back settlement. Women and men in this category are even prevented from using public transport to get about because they can't read where the tram, bus or train is going.

Parents want to understand education at all levels. They would like partnerships to develop between the teachers at their children's schools. They want to understand the education system, especially because it is provided for everyone, not just the rich. They would like some briefing sessions where the school uses Interpreters, to aid understanding.

And the Elders want people to know that they suffer terribly from isolation and subsequent loneliness. Even when they watch television, they feel excluded because of the language difficulty. The women are interested in designing the learning opportunities for their culture in partnerships with service providers.

## Current crisis

Around the 25th November 2019, nine people have died in floods in Djibouti City, capital of Djibouti, after almost a year's worth of rain fell in 2 days. The Government of Djibouti has declared a state of emergency.

News and information agency *Agence Djiboutienne d'Information (ADI)* said that 140 mm of rain fell in 48 hours from 21 November, 2019. According to WMO figures, average yearly rainfall in the city is around 164 mm.

## Numbers

Djibouti is a very small African country. It is, like Somalia, almost completely Islamic. It is incredibly difficult to discover exact numbers of refugees from Djibouti who live in Australia. Whereas Eritrea, Ethiopia are always included in the listing of Country of Origen, there is nothing for Djibouti. Somalia and South Sudan are occasionally included. In Australia, 67.3% of Australian people identify as Christian with another 24% not identifying any religion – it is not a compulsory item in the Census document. Just 2.4% identify as Muslim and Refugees from Djibouti are in this tiny percentage.

REFERENCES
floodlist.com/africa/djibouti-floods-november-2019
https://www.australia.gov.au/about-australia/our-country/our-people
https://www.everyculture.com/Cr-Ga/Djibouti.html#ixzz67ZE3Gm1Q
https://www.everyculture.com/Cr-Ga/Djibouti.html#ixzz67Z8Prl4L
https://www.expat.com/forum/696-1-everyday-life-in-djibouti.html
https://www.iexplore.com/travel-guides/africa/djibouti/history-and-culture
https://www.globalpartnership.org/country/djibouti
www.iexplore.com/articles/travel-guides%2Fafrica%2Fdjibouti%2Fattractions
https://www.lonelyplanet.com/djibouti/health
https://www.macrotrends.net/countries/DJI/djibouti/rural-population
https://www.scholaro.com/pro/countries/Djibouti/Education-system
https://www.studycountry.com/guide/DJ-education.htm
www.islamforchristians.com/islam-social-behavior
www.worldatlas.com/articles/the-culture-of-djibouti.html
www.who.int

# Eritrea

The golden wreath represents peace. This flag was adopted on December 5th, 1995. May 24 is Eritrea's Independence Day.

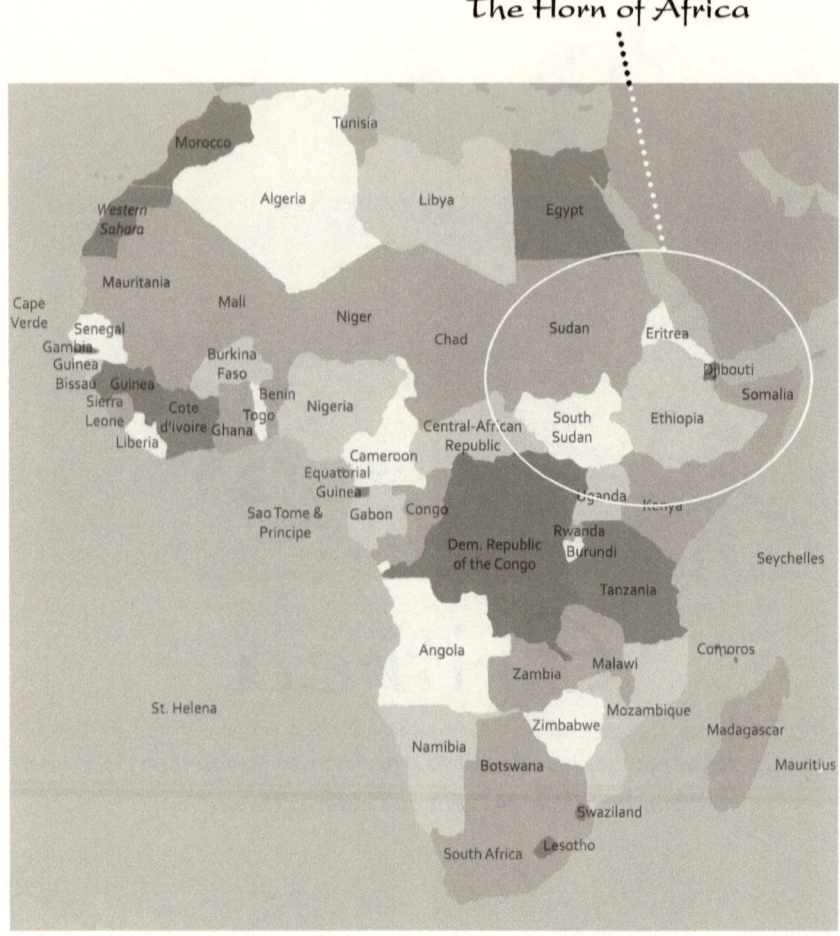

*The Horn of Africa can be seen clearly, showing the countries in this book: Djibouti, Eritrea, Ethiopia, Somalia and South Sudan, Sudan.*

# Where is Eritrea?

Eritrea is located in the Horn of Africa and is bordered on the northeast and east by the Red Sea. Off the sandy and arid coastline, the Dahlak Archipelago is situated, an archipelago with fishing grounds. The land to the south, in the highlands, is slightly less dry, and cooler. The highest point of the country, Soira, is located in the centre of Eritrea, at 3018 metres above sea level.

It is bordered by Sudan in the West, Ethiopia in the South, and Djibouti in the southeast.

Having achieved independence from Ethiopia on May 24, 1993, Eritrea is one of the youngest independent countries in Africa.

Eritreans are a very diverse people with 9 ethnic groups. Individuals may speak different first languages from one another and be of different religions. Service providers must be aware not to make generalizations about "Eritreans" and should not assume that all Eritreans with whom they work, will share the same background or information.

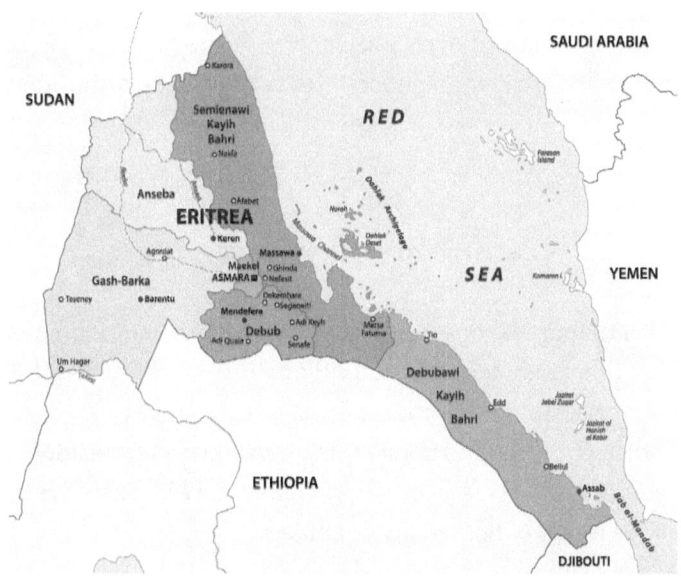

Eritreans are noted for their resilience, determination, and resourcefulness, and a strong sense of pride and independence. Eritrean women have experienced far greater equality than women from many other African countries and may therefore show greater levels of independence than women from other cultural backgrounds, qualities which assist smoother settlement experiences.

| | |
|---|---|
| Population | 5.9 million |
| Capital | Asmara |
| Area | 125,000 sq. kilometres |
| Ethnic Groups | Tigrinya, Tigre, Bilen, Afar, Saho, Kunama, Nara, Hidareb and Rashaida |
| Major languages | Tiginya, Tigre – spoken by about 80% of the population, Arabic, English |
| Major religions | Islam, Christianity |
| Life Expectancy | 51 years men, 55 years women |
| Main exports | Livestock, hides, sorghum, textiles, salt, light manufacturing |
| GNI per capita | US $180 (World Bank, 2005) This is less than half the average for Sub-Saharan Africa. |
| Main cities | Asmara, the port town of Assab in the south east, Massawa and Keren |

## Recent history in Eritrea

In 1952, the United Nations established Eritrea as an autonomous region within the Ethiopian federation, ending the British administration. A 30-year struggle for independence ended in 1991. On July 8, 2018, the two countries put an end to conflict. Eritrea's autocratic President Afwerki has led a notionally- socialist government Since 1993. The government is accused of a range of human rights abuses.

Eritrea is one of the world's poorest countries with half of the population being subject to food insecurity. Its large subsistence agriculture sector is vulnerable to drought. The country has considerable mineral wealth.

Australia's diplomatic representation is from Australia's Embassy in Cairo, Egypt.

# History

**"Victory to the Masses"**
Mass participation has become a vigorous aspect of Eritrean nation building. It was the success of the Eritrean liberation movement fighting against Ethiopia imperialism. Not only in the military field, but also in building an Eritrean "grass roots" politics of self-government. In absolute contrast with Sudan and South Sudan, with South Sudan's still raging skirmishes and civil war and the warring clans of Somalia and ethnic based liberation movements in Ethiopia, Eritrea's nine ethnic groups live in harmony and peace. There is continuing fighting with Ethiopia over border disputes in 2008 the United Nations extended the mandate of peacekeepers, some 1700 strong for 6 months. Eritrea imposed fuel restrictions in the border areas. Ethiopia refused to accept a binding international Court of Justice ruling on the border. The UN was forced out.

High levels of popular participation in the country's reconstruction and development are the hallmarks of Eritrea's post-independence growth. At the same time, instances of crime or corruption have remained lower than many other countries. This speaks to the high levels of social cohesion and civic pride that under gird the social and economic development process.

The National Service (NSP), written into Eritrea's Constitution as an obligation of citizenship, requires all women and men over 18 to undergo 6 months of military training and a year of work on national reconstruction. The value of the NSP is that it compensates for Eritrea's lack of capital and reduces Eritrea's dependence on foreign aid, while welding together Eritrea's diverse society. It also places women in a condition of heightened gender equality for 18 months, as service in the NSP has done during Eritrea's war of independence.

In September 2017, the Eritrean Foreign Minister spoke to the UN. He said talk of an "African renaissance" was misplaced. He complained that Eritrea had suffered unfairly by the UN imposed sanctions since 2008. He also said that Ethiopia had to end its 15 year occupation of Eritrean territory.

## UN sanctions

Since 1996 the UN has imposed 30 sanctions regimes – Eritrea, Ethiopia, Sudan, South Sudan are included. Sanctions include arms embargoes, travel bans, financial and commodity restrictions.

Eritrea

# The Diaspora

With more than one million Eritreans living "in exile", according to the government, and a population of close to 6 million citizens, a high percentage of citizens live abroad or in nearby countries, such as north Sudan. Young people were sent away for fear of forced conscription into Ethiopia's army and to avert the daily cruelties of the 1961 – 1991 Ethiopian occupation. The majority of the exiles walked, some for hundreds of miles to north Sudan. Around half million still live there. Another 250,000 are scattered around the world. Eritreans remain staunchly loyal to their motherland and their families. These exiles raised much of the financial support for the 30-year liberation struggle, and faithfully continue to assist family members back home, monetarily and materially.

There are approximately 4,116 Eritreans living in Melbourne, which is 65.1% of all the Eritreans in Australia. There are members of Islam plus several Christian churches. Speak with an Eritrean and you will be told the same things about the respect that each religious group has for the others and that is quite different to many other multiethnic religions in Australia. They are Eritreans first and religious second.

# General

Eritrea is one of the youngest nations in Africa and contains remnants of its oldest Civilizations. Eritrea fought and won one of the longest wars in the world. After 30 yearsOf bitter struggle, Eritrea achieved total independence and the right to self-determination. The Eritrean people achieved their goals in 1991 in a stunning defeat of the occupying Ethiopian forces.

Eritrea is a multi-ethnic country, with nine recognized ethnic groups in its population of around 6 million.

## Early History

Between 1000 and 400 BC, a Semitic group of people called the Sabeans crossed the Red Sea into the region now known as Eritrea, and intermingled with the Hamitic inhabitants who had migrated from the Northern Sudan. The region as then controlled by various foreign invaders such as the Axumite kingdom, the Funji Sultans of Sudan, the Egyptians, the Portuguese and the Turks. Each of these foreign occupiers had a distinct impact on the development of modern-day Eritrea.

## Colonisation: Italy 1880 – 1941

This was the era during which Eritrea emerged as a distinct society and territory. In the 1880s Italy purchased the Port of Assab from a commercial company which was administering it.

Italy moved to transform Eritrea, with its access to sea and agricultural potential, into a colony. On January 1, 1890, the King of Italy declared Eritrea a Nation State and a colony of Italy. In the 1930s, about 70,000 Italians lived there.

As the agricultural production was intended for the benefit of the settlement population, infrastructure was developed. The Italians built railway lines between Asmara and Keren and Agordat. The Port of Massawa was linked by rail to the interior. All weather roads were constructed through the mountains of Eritrea and the lowlands. Two modern airports were built. An export based industrial sector was created and Eritrea forged new links with the international economy.

In contrast, Ethiopia stayed as a feudal economic system, managed by imperial rule.

Eritrea evolved a substantial working class as well as a distinct urban-based intelligentsia. The Italian rule was not, however, benign. Eritrea's people were seen merely as a source of cheap labour to fuel the aims of Rome. Eritreans played only a small part in their country's economic development.

## Great Britain's role

With the defeat of Italy in 1941, the great powers – France, Soviet Union, UK and US, decided that Britain would govern Eritrea as a protectorate. This was viewed by Eritreans as preferable to the Italian occupation, and coincided with the first signs of Eritrean nationalism. Peasant resistance had already been experienced.

In Ethiopia, the newly reinstated Ethiopian Emperor, began to try increasing his influence over Eritrea through the tactics of interference in religious affairs, manipulation of political parties and organisations and terrorism.

## UN decides Eritrea's fate

With the end of World War 11 came United Nations oversight of Eritrea. The US were showing interest in maintaining a strategic presence on the Red Sea. The British were finding it becoming difficult to manage Ethiopia. Ethiopia was staking a claim to Eritrea. Discussions which would decide the fate of Eritrea began in 1949 in New York. On December 2, 1950, the UN passed a resolution that formally federated Eritrea to Ethiopia, even though the British reported that 75% of the population supported independence.

## Liberation Struggle 1961 – 1991

Although there was organized resistance throughout the British Military Administration and federation with Ethiopia, the first act of armed resistance by Eritreans against Ethiopian rule was 1961. The Ethiopians retaliated by totally annexing Eritrea in 1992. Scattered resistance groups formed links with pro-independence movements outside the country. This led to the formation of the Eritrean Liberation Front and in 1965 there were about 1,000 fighters in the field. By the late 1976, there were 20,000 fighters in the field. The Eritrean Peoples Liberation Front (EPLF), became skilled and effective fighters and they were able to recapture 90% of Eritrea from a demoralized Ethiopian army by 1990. The EPLF established networks of underground hospitals, factories, schools, libraries for the benefit of the people in liberated zones. Literacy and public health campaigns significantly improved the daily lives of peasant farmers. The EPLF instituted civil administration, legal and social codes that transformed the traditional and colonial structures that preceded them.

Marriage, property and inheritance customs were re-vamped to provide equality for historically oppressed Eritrean women. More than 30% of the EPLF fighters were women.

# The Birth of a Nation

On the 23rd – 25th April 1993, a United Nations Referendum was held. And formal independence was declared on 24 May 1993. Eritrea's independence was recognized by the world. This has left Ethiopia landlocked, as their access to the Eritrean ports of Massawa and Assab is blocked.

# President

Isaias Aferwerki was elected President of the independent Eritrea by the country's national assembly in 1993. He had been the de facto leader before independence.

Presidential elections, planned for 1997, were never held. Eritrea remains a one-party State, with the ruling People's Front for democracy and Justice the only party allowed to operate.

Mr Aferwerki has been criticized for failing to implement democratic reforms. His government has clamped down on its critics and closed the private press. Born in 1946 in Asmara, Isaias Afewerki joined the ELF in 1966. He received military training in China the same year, then went on to be deputy divisional commander. In 1970 he co-founded the Eritrean Peoples Liberation Front (EPLF) and in 1987 he was elected secretary-general of the organization.

## Ongoing fighting and challenges

In 1989 border disputes erupted into open hostilities. This resulted in the deaths of thousands of soldiers from both countries, and subjected Eritrea to significant economic and social stresses, including massive population displacement, reduced economic development, and one of Africa's more severe landmine problems.

This conflict ended with a formal treaty in 2000. A security zone, patrolled by the United Nations separates the two countries. As of October 2005, the border question remains in dispute.

This border dispute is compounded by other problems. These include Eritrea's inability to provide enough food; two thirds of the population receive food aid. The economic progress is hampered by the proportion of Eritreans who are in the army, rather than in the workforce.

As well as Eritrea being a one-party State, no group larger than 7 is allowed to assemble without government approval. Elections were cancelled in 1997 and again in 2001. Regional elections were held, but the officials hold little power.

# Religions

The Eritrean government has enforced the Italian colonial practice of requiring government approval of all practiced religions. Currently approved religions are the Eritrean Orthodox Church, the Roman Catholic Church, the Eritrean Mekane Yesus Evangelical Lutheran Church and Islam. All other sects in general and fundamentalist Evangelical Protestant Christians in particular, were suppressed across the country.

Christianity and Islam each represent about 50% of the population The main Christian group was in full communion with the Egyptian and Ethiopian Coptic Christian churches. In 1998 the Archbishop of Asmara, the young nation's capital was elevated to the rank of Patriarchate of Eritrea, within the Coptic church.

The vast majority of Muslims in Eritrea are Sunni Muslims.

Despite contrasts between the Muslim and Christian religions and the potential for conflict, both religious groups have lived together in harmony and peace. This is something unusual and a characteristic of Eritreans about which they are justifiably proud.

## Religion and health issues
From: www.islam-usa.com/e40.html

- Cleanliness is considered "half of the faith". Qur'an, the holy book, prohibits eating pork or pork products, meat of dead animals, blood and all intoxicants.
- Respect a Muslim's modesty and privacy. Some health examinations can be done over a gown. Provide same sex health care persons, if possible. Always examine a female patient in the presence of another female.
- Some Muslim men will not shake a woman's hand.
- Provide Muslim or Kosher meals.
- Allow them to pray, and if they can read, to read the Qur'an.
- Take time to explain medical tests, procedures and treatment.
- During a birthing, it is preferred that the father be the sole male present.

There is also a range of deep cultural beliefs and attitudes in Muslim communities towards disability that need to be discussed. They are:
- A social stigma with corresponding fear of "visibility" in the community.
- A curse or punishment for some wrongdoing. This belief is evident among other cultures, such as north Sudanese.
- A gift from God or God-given, when a disadvantaged child or person is seen as a blessing.

# Christian and Muslim families

Family is the foundation of Eritrean society. The peace and security offered by a stable family unit is greatly valued and is seen as essential for the spiritual growth of its members. A harmonious social order is created by the existence of extended families. Children are treasured, and rarely leave home until they marry.

# Christians, Muslims and the Elderly

In Eritrea there are no old peoples' homes. The practice of caring for one's elderly relatives is considered an honour and blessing, and an opportunity for great spiritual growth. God asks that we pray for our parents, but act

with limitless compassion, remembering that when we were helpless little children, they preferred to help us rather than themselves.

Mothers are particularly respected in both religions. The Prophet Mohammed said "Paradise lies at the feet of mothers".

When they reach old age, Eritrean parents are treated mercifully, with kindness and selflessness. Serving one's parents is a duty second only to prayer, and it is their right to expect it. It is considered despicable to express any irritation, if an old person becomes difficult.

Respite care and nursing homes may be used. Hospitals are also acceptable to many, however people without English are frightened about remaining in mainstream institutions.

## Communication of diagnosis/prognosis in a medical situation

News of an illness is first given to the family – the closest member to the patient. The next of kin will advise the immediate family, but perhaps advice will not be given to friends.

Patients are often not told about a life-threatening disease, as it is felt that to do so might make their condition worse. They also may be ostracized by their community because people may consider them infectious and/or cursed.

Every family is different. Plus, after being in a western country for several years, the understanding of English could be fairly good, so it might be possible to tell the person gently about the diagnosis. If a patient wants to know, tell him/her.

In some cases, the family leaves all the telling to the medical staff, in other families, the wisest person will manage the telling.

Words like "dying" and "cancer" are used with sensitivity, as for any group. Cancer is sometimes referred to as "That Disease". Avoid discussing death, dying and how long a person is likely to live.

When a person is dying, family and friends are called in to stay until the person passes away. The Qur'an is recited until they pass away. Once the person has died, the house is open, and condolences are received. There are no celebrations or frivolities. Burial and religious rites are performed within 24 hours.

# Role and acceptable behaviors of health professionals/volunteers

For a Muslim, it would be preferable that treating professionals are the same gender as the patient.

Visitors to a Muslim home should be aware that alcoholic drinks are not permitted. Pork in any form is not permitted. Mostly, the meat should be Halal; that is slaughtered in a special way with a sharp knife and prayers in the name of Allah.

Health professionals need to be aware of the need for people to wash and pray 5 times a day.

# Attitudes to pain relief

There are no taboos for pain relief for Christians or Muslims. Check whether medicines contain alcohol.

# Information provision

Written material will be useful to those who can read. About 25% of the population is literate. Ask the family who to give the printed information to.

Other effective strategies are meetings, forums, community education. Arabic newspapers, radio and TV is better than free to air TV.

## Settlement Issues

There are about 5,000 Eritreans living in Australia. Of these 3,000 – 4,000 live in Melbourne.

- **Number of single mothers:** due to men being killed, or reported missing, during the war women with or without children are alone. Many of the women from rural areas are illiterate on arrival.
- **Housing:** there is difficulty finding appropriate housing for families, as the number of children can be large for Australia. Private rental is expensive and difficult to achieve due to their not having a rental history in Australia.
- **Changing family roles:** lack of role models, particularly male, for youth has led to attitude and behavioural problems. Men find it difficult to secure employment and become frustrated and humiliated, as traditionally men are the financial providers in Eritrea. Women work hard to keep the home running as they did in Eritrea. They are used to making the best out of challenging situations and do a lot to help the family settle in comparatively quickly.
- **Family separation:** causes feelings of grief and loneliness amongst families. Separation also increases pressure on families as there is no extended family to look after children in Australia.
- **Inter-generational conflict:** particularly between the youth and the elderly as the young generation are adapting to an Australian lifestyle, often rejecting their Eritrean culture.
- **Racism:** The Eritrean community believes that racist attitudes can affect them in securing employment, housing and other opportunities.
- **Emotional wellbeing:** mental health – it is felt by Eritreans, that this is an area of greatest need and health problems. Depression, anxiety, post-traumatic stress disorder is an increasing problem, due to torture, traumas which have been experienced by every new arrival. Then there is culture shock and the pressures of settling in Australia. Eritreans are not shy about accessing help from professionals, which

is different to refugees from other African groups who are suspicious of new services.
- **Physical disability:** due to strict laws regarding the health of refugees who are accepted into Australia, there is not a high incidence of physically disabled Eritreans here. There are some war injuries, but mostly these Eritreans have gone to Belgium.
- **Literacy and language:** It is important to be aware that there may be literacy issues with newly arrived refugees. The use of Interpreters is highly valued and makes a service provider's life easier, in that information is understood quickly.

## Nutrition for women

Information from: Ecology of Food and Nutrition, 2004, vol.43, no.3, pp.213 – 229. Cate Burns. Publisher: Taylor and Francis Ltd.

## Women

Eritrean women played a central role in liberating the nation in 1991 and in defending it when it came under renewed Ethiopian attack in 1998 – 2000. Because of the important role women played in the society and economy, the Eritrean government has sought to ensure their full and equal participation while eliminating the disadvantages that many of the women experience. The National Union of Eritrean Women (NUEW) with its 200,000 members is an umbrella organization upholding the rights of Eritrean women throughout Eritrea and the Diaspora and securing woman's participation in the Eritrean society.

## Cuisine of Eritrea

**Igni** – meat with chilli, Shiro – pea soup, Injera – flat bread made of wheat or sorghum and hibet – paste made from legumes, mainly lentil and faba beans.

Recipe: Alitcha Birsen

Ingredients: 3 Tablespoons sunflower or other vegetable oil
6 cloves of garlic, crushed
250 gms lentils
1 teaspoon salt
1 teaspoon black pepper
1 teaspoon ginger
2 fresh red chilies – remove the seeds. Don't rub your eyes!
1 litre water

Heat the oil in a pan and fry the garlic light brown. Add sliced tomatoes. Simmer 5 minutes. Add washed lentils, simmer. Add salt, pepper, ginger, chilli and boiling water. Simmer covered for one hour. Serve with Injera.

## Tsebhi sega – spicy minced meat

Ingredients:
2 medium sized onions, chopped
2 Tablespoons sunflower or other vegetable oil
Chilli paste to taste – homemade berbere is really delicious, so don't skimp as this is about flavour as well as heat
1 or 2 Tablespoons tegelese tesmi
1 teaspoon chopped ginger
1 teaspoon chopped garlic
6 large tomatoes, skinned
1 kilo beef or lamb, shredded (minced)
Pepper and salt to taste.

Heat the oil in a frying pan and fry the onions light golden brown. Add the berbere and the tegelese tesmi and some water if necessary and simmer it on a low fire. Add the ginger and the garlic after 10 minutes and the sliced, skinned tomatoes, some salt and pepper for another 15 minutes. Add the meat and simmer it until the meat is done. Add some water if necessary. Serve with Injera.

REFERENCES

DIMIA 2000 Immigration Update. June quarter
Gordon F.L. 2000, Ethiopia, Eritrea and Djibouti. Lonely Planet Publications, Melbourne.
http://denbe.asmarino.com/asmarino/Eritrea
http://www.abs.gov.au/ausstats
http://news.bbc.co.uk/hi/english/word/africa/newsid_784000/784347.stm
http://www.australia.gov.au/about-australia/our-country/our-people
http://www.cia.gov/cia/publications/factbook/geos/er.html
http://www.ethnologue.com
http://www.refugees.org/world/countryrpt/Africa/Eritrea.htm

# Ethiopia

*Independence Day May 24*

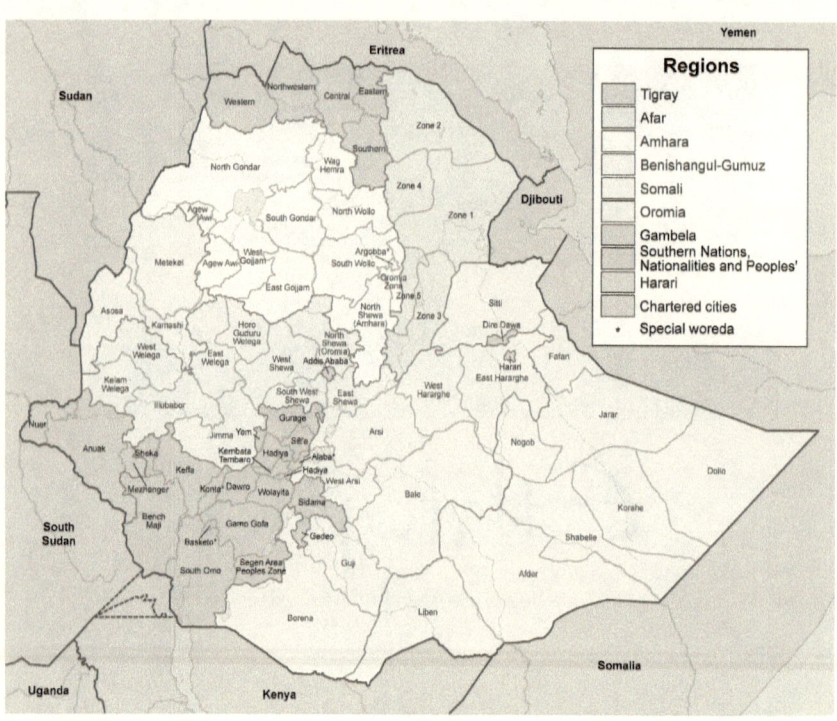

# Ethiopia

Ethiopia is a large African country situated in the Horn of Africa, bordering Sudan, South Sudan, Kenya, Somalia, Eritrea and Djibouti. The country has the second biggest population in Africa, with over 50% of people being under 25 years of age.1 Due to the vast size of the population, it is important to recognise that descriptions of Ethiopian cultural customs can vary significantly.

> "Ethiopia is the oldest independent country in Africa, Founded in 980 B.C. once ruled as a dynasty by a series of monarchs. It is distinct from most other African nations as it is one of the only countries that successfully resisted European colonisation. It also has a historical connection to Christianity, with the region adopting the religion before many Western nations were exposed to it"
>
> (SBS, November, 2019).

Ethiopians have one of the lowest life expectancies in the world. Current figures estimate that women can expect to live for about 50 years, and men for about 48 years.

Throughout its history, there have been many wars and battles where rulers have been ousted and people forced to flee. Ethiopia, unlike Somalia, Eritrea and South Sudan, has looked to other nations for help, such as the Russian and Italians.

Ethiopia is land locked these days, with Djibouti having access to the Red Sea and the Gulf of Aden.

## Prehistory

For most of its history, Ethiopia has had a long series of Emperors. Even as far back as the 2nd millennium BC, it was a monarchy, first founded in 980BC. Today the population is more than 105 million people

Ethiopia has been occupied for possibly the longest time able to be verified. The oldest hominid is 4.2 million years old, discovered in 1994. Another famous hominid is "Lucy", discovered in 1974. She is estimated to be 3.2 million years old.

Ethiopia is also thought to be one of the world's earliest places where Homosapiens lived. Some bones are two and three hundred thousand years old. It is thought these people came out of the Nile Valley, which fits with the history claimed by the South Sudanese.

In 2019, archaeologists discovered a 300,000 year old rock shelter, in Ethiopia's mountains at an elevation of 3,469 metres. This is proof that very ancient people could live at this high altitude.

## Antiquity

Hundreds of years go by with new Emperors replacing older Emperors and Empires being established and lost. Some civlisations lived in both Ethiopia and Eritrea. A coin dated 324 AD shows that Ethiopia was the second country to adopt Christianity, although this claim is not proven. The Axumite dynasty was just after Armenia adopted it in 301 AD. Muslims came in 614AD. Around 912AD, Islam was accepted in Ethiopia.

This claim is being challenged, which would upset millions of Christian Ethiopians. There is an argument that Armenia was not the first country, and that Christianity actually came first to the Abyssinian country, which was made up of Ethiopia and Eritrea. The book, written by Brendon Pringle in 2013, says that St. Gregory baptized the Armenium king, King Trdat III in 301/304AD. A 5th century book excerpt claimed that the author, Agathangelos said he was an eyewitness. Recently this book was dated to 450AD, making it impossible to be true.

*Coins from the third century AD.*

Ethiopia has a different background story, recorded in the Acts of the Apostles of an incident shortly after the death of Christ. Eusebius of Caesaria, the first church historian, tells of how a eunuch was baptized after the Resurrection and before the arrival of Apostle Matthew (Pringle, 2013)

## Middle Ages:

Early 15th century Ethiopia made diplomatic contact with Europe. The first continuous relationship was with Portugal in 1508. In 1624, the Emperor declared Ethiopia's religion to be Ethiopian Orthodoxy. He expelled Catholic, Jesuit priests and other Europeans.

Ethiopian Muslims arrived in Ethiopia after the Prophet Mohammed sent 11 men and 5 women to Megash, where the King ruled and let them in. It is said that Mohammed sent his daughter but she later went back to Mecca. The 1st mosque built is in the process of being renovated so it can be listed on the World Heritage listing. There is a temple in Yaha built of limestone. Its treasures are kept nearby. A great palace was built before the 8th century. Yaha was very significant as a capital city.

*19th century Emperors Tewodros II and Yohannes IV*

Between 1755 and 1855, Ethiopia had a period of isolation. This ended after Britain concluded an alliance, but it took till 1855 to completely unite the tribes and clans. During this period, Turkey invaded twice.

From 1889–1913 it was a period of many changes as rulers came and went. Battles were fought where thousands died. In 1889, Ethiopia signed a Treaty with Italy, who in turn asked for some land north of Ethiopia in modern day Eritrea. The Italians spread out further and the war ended in 1896 when Ethiopia beat the Italians.

*The 17th century castle of Fasilides*

This is a second major contentious issue for Ethiopia. Ethiopia claims to have never been colonized by any country, despite Italy being in charge briefly and Britain being resident in the country. Britain pushed the then King Theodore off his throne, but the plan failed, and Britain virtually said Ethiopia was not worth the effort. Italy tried a couple of times after this, with Italian troops invading Ethiopia. Their move failed because around 100,000 troops beat Italy at the Battle of Adwa in 1896. European countries also recognized Ethiopia as a sovereign state. In World War 11, Benito Mussolini tried again but ultimately, he failed and so Ethiopia claims to have never been a colony of any country.

1916 – 1974: Emperor Haile Selassie ruled. 1935 was another war with Italy. Italy won this war and began to build infrastructure for Ethiopia, like roads and buildings. But in 1937, Italians massacred Ethiopians. From 1935 – 41, Ethiopia was under Italian occupation. Eritrea and Ethiopia united in a federation. Then the Eritrean Independence war occurred. The Emperor was overthrown in 1974. In 1977 Somalia invaded but was pushed back.

There was a famine in 1984 that killed one million people and a 30-year civil war occurred up to 1991 against Eritrea. Ethiopia remains impoverished, but its economy is growing at one of the world's fastest rates.

Ethiopians and Eritreans both generally identify as 'habesha'*. This term is used to describe the unique culture and people of the Ethiopian/Eritrean region, regardless of ethnicity. This is quite unusual and the complete opposite of neighbouring countries, such as South Sudan which remains divided along tribal groupings.

## Major challenges

There are major problems facing Ethiopia today. Environmental issues such as water pollution as a result of agricultural and industrial runoffs, land degradation which often leads to desertification, poor climatic conditions including severe droughts, continue to threaten lives in Ethiopia today.

Ethnic, religious and political violence has marred the 21st century. Many battles and skirmishes have been fought and one result has been the strengthening of Islam in the region.

*Adigrat in north Ethiopia*

1.4 million people fled their homes in 2018, and South Sudan would also be noted as having more than 1 million people displaced. Ethiopia has suffered by continuous warfare throughout history, mainly with the ethnic groups of Ethiopia itself.

In 2019, religion in Ethiopia consists of a number of faiths. Among these mainly Abrahamic religions, the most numerous is Christianity (Ethiopian Orthodoxy, Pentay, Catholic) totaling at 62.8%, followed by Islam at 33.9%. There is also a longstanding but small Jewish community. Figures from the 1994 census. (Britannica 2019)

## The United Nations

Ethiopia is a strong supporter of the United Nations Security Council and has participated in a number of peacekeeping missions to countries including Congo, Liberia, Rwanda, Burundi and Korea. Ethiopia's main focus at the United Nations currently pertains to social and economic issues, along with maintaining security and peace worldwide.

The United Nations Country Team (UNCT) in Ethiopia is the largest UN Country Team in Africa, comprising of twenty-five members. UNCT along with the UN System supports the Government of Ethiopia's developmental priorities along with a wide range of projects and programs including:

Food security
Agricultural programs
Capacity building
Environmental issues
Industry
Education
Emergency relief
Humanitarian activities
Health
Civil service reform

The United Nations Volunteer Program (UNV) was launched in Ethiopia in 1970 to promote poverty reduction strategies and develop support services. The United Nations Economic Commission for Africa's headquarters are located in Nairobi and Ethiopia.

## National Identity and Pride

It is common to encounter quite patriotic views among Ethiopians. Many feel their country has great cultural depth and wealth in comparison to others. For example, there is a general expectation that an Ethiopian living overseas will eventually want to return or stay connected to their country (regardless of improved living circumstances elsewhere) as their culture is incomparable.

Ethiopians also share a deep pride in the country's legacy and what it symbolizes as an historically independent African nation. The Ethiopian Empire (also known as Abyssinia) was one of the last active empires in the world. Its strong statehood was a key to Ethiopia's successful resis-

tance of colonisation.5 The fact that the culture claims to be untouched by colonialism is a massive source of pride for Ethiopians. (culturalatlas.sbs.com.au)

## Greetings

Greetings are very important in Ethiopia. It is expected that people acknowledge one another courteously even if they do not speak the same language.

It is rude to rush through a greeting or pass by someone without acknowledging them even briefly.

Greet the eldest people first out of respect.

It is common to shake hands to greet strangers, using the right hand or both hands. Make eye contact during a handshake. However, this should be the only assertive aspect of the interaction. People generally hold one another's hands quite lightly.

## Family and Housing

The extended family often lives together, so aunts, uncles, even close friends share a home. The family's priorities come before those of individuals.

Having some animals is considered very important – "if you don't have some animals, one cannot survive". (Africa-expert.com/ethiopia/family-and-housing, Nov. 2019)

The Dassanach people of southern Ethiopia and the Omo valley have seminomadic migration patterns that relates to the rain and greener pastures for their livestock, so their houses are not built to be permanent structures in the landscape, but merely as periodical shelters.

A house is usually round and made of mudbricks, unlike the tree branches of the Dassanach people's home above, then fitted with a grass roof, see below.

*Ethiopia*

In towns and cities, houses are usually walled constructions" fitted with a fixed metal or mud roof. "In Addis, the newest trends in architecture …. creates a fascinating mix. "Architecture reflects Ethiopia's cultural diversity" (Africa-expert.com…Nov. 2019)

## Religion and health issues
From: www.islam-usa.com/e40.html

- Cleanliness is considered "half of the faith". Qur'an, the holy book, prohibits eating pork or pork products, meat of dead animals, blood and all intoxicants.
- Respect a Muslim's modesty and privacy. Some health examinations can be done over a gown. Provide same sex health care persons, if possible. Always examine a female patient in the presence of another female.
- Some Muslim men will not shake a woman's hand.
- Provide Muslim or Kosher meals.

*Community health care workers.*

- Allow them to pray, and if they can read, to read the Qur'an.
- Take time to explain medical tests, procedures and treatment.
- During a birthing, it is preferred that the father be the sole male present.

There is also a range of deep cultural beliefs and attitudes in Muslim communities towards disability that need to be discussed. They are:
- A social stigma with corresponding fear of "visibility" in the community.
- A curse or punishment for some wrongdoing. This belief is evident among other cultures, such as north Sudanese.
- A gift from God or God-given, when a disadvantaged child or person is seen as a blessing.

## Christian and Muslim families

Family is the foundation of Ethiopian society. The peace and security offered by a stable family unit is greatly valued and is seen as essential for the spiritual growth of its members. A harmonious social order is created by the existence of extended families. Children are treasured, and rarely leave home until they marry.

## Christians, Muslims and the Elderly

In Ethiopia, there are no old peoples' homes. The practice of caring for one's elderly relatives is considered an honour and blessing, and an opportunity for great spiritual growth. God asks that we pray for our parents, but act with limitless compassion, remembering that when we were helpless little children, they preferred to help us rather than themselves.

Mothers are particularly respected in both religions. The Prophet Mohammed said "Paradise lies at the feet of mothers".

When they reach old age, Ethiopian parents are treated mercifully, with kindness and selflessness. Serving one's parents is a duty second only to prayer, and it is their right to expect it. It is considered despicable to express any irritation, if an old person becomes difficult.

Respite care and nursing homes may be used. Hospitals are also acceptable to many, however people without English are frightened about remaining in mainstream institutions.

## Communication of diagnosis/prognosis in a medical situation

News of an illness is first given to the family – the closest member to the patient. The next of kin will advise the immediate family, but perhaps advice will not be given to friends.

Patients are often not told about a life-threatening disease, as it is felt that to do so might make their condition worse. They also may be

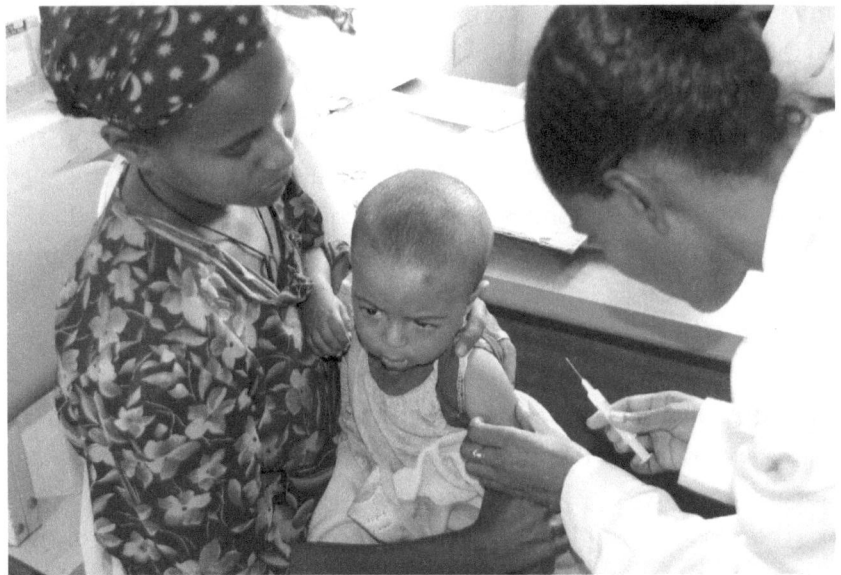

ostracized by their community because people may consider them infectious and/or cursed.

Every family is different. Plus, after being in a western country for several years, the understanding of English could be fairly good, so it might be possible to tell the person gently about the diagnosis. If a patient wants to know, tell him/her.

In some cases, the family leaves all the telling to the medical staff, in other families, the wisest person will manage the telling.

Words like "dying" and "cancer" are used with sensitivity, as for any group. Cancer is sometimes referred to as "That Disease". Avoid discussing death, dying and how long a person is likely to live.

When a person is dying, family and friends are called in to stay until the person passes away. The Qur'an is recited until they pass away. Once the person has died, the house is open, and condolences are received. There are no celebrations or frivolities. Burial and religious rites are performed within 24 hours.

## Government areas of responsibility

### Health in Ethiopia

USAID has a huge holistic program of support, food, knowledge and service provision. This is in the face of "twenty-two percent of Ethiopian women malnourished, and 38 percent of children suffering from chronic under-nutrition" (UN,2019). In conjunction with the Feed the Future Initiative and other USAID programs, we provide technical assistance in developing national policy, programs, guidelines, and improving the quality and access to essential health and nutrition services. USAID works with hospitals and health centers in Ethiopia to provide nutritional assessments and counseling support, as well as providing fortification and nutritional supplements to undernourished children".

The World Health Organization's 2006 World Health Report gives a figure of 1,936 physicians for 2003, which comes to about 2.6 per 100,000. There is a move by some doctors to leave and go to a western country.

Ethiopia has 12 deaths per thousand for children aged 5 – 12 years, this is much fewer than South Sudan, or Somalia.

Numbers for Disability adjusted deaths in 2012 were 21,724 people, which makes Ethiopia number 99 out of 174 countries. They are behind Sudan, Eritrea and Somalia.

(Nationmaster.com, Nov, 2019)

**Education**

There are 8 years of compulsory education, just as there are in Australia. One would suppose that this might mean Australia education is not as daunting for Ethiopian children as for children who might never have been to school, such as South Sudan.

> "The education system in Ethiopia is divided into three divisions consisting of primary school, lower secondary school, and higher secondary school. The primary schooling lasts for 6 years, the lower secondary 4 years, and the higher secondary 2 years. Elementary education is usually taught in the local languages especially in the rural areas.
>
> (studycountry.com, Nov, 2019)

Education in Ethiopia is compulsory for children between the ages of 5 to 16, but with poor facilities and underprivileged backgrounds, many children do not get a high quality, full-time education, despite the large majority of teachers being trained. But sometimes with a class size of 100 students, learning and teaching must suffer.

Poor governance and corruption are major problems in almost all African countries. Most political figures in Ethiopia today are very corrupt with little or no experience at all. "Poor governance and political instability in Ethiopia also drives investors away".

## Infrastructure

**Economy**
**Energy and hydropower**
Ethiopia has 14 major rivers flowing from its highlands, including the Nile. It has the largest water reserves in Africa. As of 2012, hydroelectric plants represented around 88.2% of the total installed electricity generating capacity.

Agriculture constitutes around 85% of the labour force. However, the service sector represents the largest portion of the GDP. Many other economic activities depend on agriculture, including marketing, processing, and export of agricultural products.

Exports from Ethiopia in the 2009/2010 financial year totaled US$1.4 billion. The country produces more coffee than any other nation on the continent." Coffee provides a livelihood for close to 15 million Ethiopians, 16% of the population.

## Settlement issues in Ethiopia
https://www.britannica.com/place/Ethiopia/Settlement-patterns

Ethiopian Settlement patterns: With only about one-fifth of the population urbanized, most Ethiopians live in scattered rural communities. In order to reduce traveling distance, homesteads are generally scattered to be near farm plots. Therefore, settlement into Australia is vastly different for Ethiopians.

## Migration history

Ethiopian refugees who would eventually settle in Australia began flowing out of their home country as early as the 1970s, when the Derg, a military leadership, came to power. They lived in refugee camps in neighbouring countries, mainly Sudan and Kenya, some for as long as 20 years before they found a country willing to resettle them.

## Ethiopian Australians

Due to inter-ethnic tensions some former refugees call themselves according to a geographic name, such as Oromo Australians.
Total population in Australia:
5,600 (by ancestry, 2006)
5,633 (by birth, 2006).

According to the 2011 Census, 51.3 per cent of Ethiopia-born Australians 15 years and over in age had some form of higher non-school qualifications. 19.7 per cent of the Ethiopia-born aged 15 years and over were still attending an educational institution.[9]

Ethiopia-born individuals in Australia aged 15 years and over participated in the labour force at a rate of 62.3 per cent; the unemployment rate was 15 per cent. Of the 3,775 Ethiopia-born immigrants who were employed, 26.2 per cent worked in a professional, skilled managerial or trade occupation.

The vast majority of Ethiopians living in Australia today have arrived since 2000. This includes people of all education and skill levels, ages and genders. Approximately 3,000 arrived between 2000 and 2005. The majority of these individuals arrived on humanitarian visas (65%) or family visas (33%). Many were single or widowed mothers and their children. The Australian government granted a further 1,345 humanitarian visas to Ethiopia-born refugees between 2012 and 2017. Again, the majority of these refugees arrived from surrounding countries (such as Sudan and Kenya).

AMES Australia has been providing settlement services to newly arrived refugees and humanitarian entrants since 2005. Between October 2005 and June 2017, AMES Australia assisted over 51,000 clients with their settlement across Victoria; close to 20,000 under Integrated Humanitarian Settlement Strategy (IHSS) between October 2005 and March 2011 and over 21,000 clients assisted through Humanitarian Settlement Services (HSS) from April 2011 until June 2017. AMES delivers 510 hours of English per person.

From October 2017, AMES Australia (alongside consortium partners and sub-contractors) began delivering the Humanitarian Settlement Program (HSP) in Victoria, South Australia and Tasmania.

HSP is funded by the Australian Government Department of Home Affairs.

## Settlement in Australia

According to the 2006 Australian census 5,633 Australians were born in Ethiopia while 5,600 claimed Ethiopian ancestry, either alone or with another ancestry. The similar figures for ancestry and place of birth are indicative of the very recent immigration of this group.

Australia's 2001 census found about 3,600 residents of the country who reported their place of birth as Ethiopia. This made them the 15th-largest group of Ethiopian-born people in a country outside of Ethiopia, ahead of the United Arab Emirates and behind Norway. About 85% of those lived in Melbourne,

According to the 2011 Census, 51.3 per cent of Ethiopia-born Australians 15 years and over in age had some form of higher non-school qualifications. 19.7 per cent of the Ethiopia-born aged 15 years and over were still attending an educational institution.

Ethiopia-born individuals in Australia aged 15 years and over participated in the labour force at a rate of 62.3 per cent; the unemployment rate was 15 per cent. Of the 3,775 Ethiopia-born immigrants who were employed, 26.2 per cent worked in a professional, skilled managerial or trade occupation. In Footscray, some have set up ethnic-oriented businesses, such as hair salons, clothing shops, and restaurants with a mostly Ethiopian customer base. These tend to be very successful businesses.

REFERENCES
africa-expert.com/ethiopia/family-and-housing, Nov. 2019
Encyclopedia Britannica,
https://www.britannica.com/place/Ethiopia/Settlement-patterns viewed 25/11/2019
https://www.ames.net.au/settle-in-aus/humanitarian-settlement-program
https://dfat.gov.au/geo/ethiopia
https://www.nationmaster.com/country-info/profiles/Ethiopia/Health/Health-services
SBS Cultural Atlas, November, 2019
culturalatlas.sbs.com.au/ethiopian-culture/core-concepts-5edb1a3c-13b8-4b5f-84e1-cd-081b30e100#core-concepts-5edb1a3c-13b8-4b5f-84e1-cd081b30e100:
www.studycountry.com/guide/ET-education.htm

# Oromo

*An Introduction
to the Oromo people and culture.*

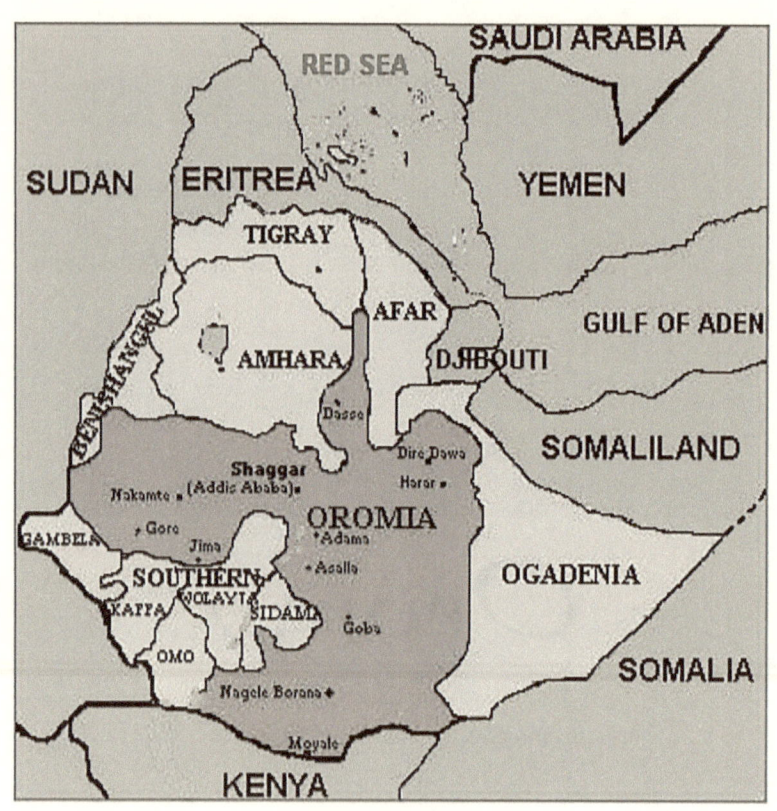

Map of Oramia

The fundamental political objective of Oromians is to achieve national self-determination, and to liberate themselves form more than a century of oppression.

The Oromo peoples' lives are marked with war, as a result of having once been a free country, until Abyssinia occupied territory at the end of the 19th Century. There have been genocidal size attacks and displacement of over a million people.

The area of Oromia is rich in natural elements, animals, forests, water. Agriculture is the main occupation for Oromo people. Over 90% of its people are pastoralists. Their main crops are coffee and Khat a mild stimulating shrub.

Currently, Oromia is classified as being part of the Unrepresented Nations and Peoples' Organisation. Starting the process in 2009, the Oromia Support Group Australia (OSGA) received special consultation status, a significant achievement for the NGO. The process began in 2009. Diaspora Action Australia kept helping them.

This status allows OSGA to attend the UN's group for economic and Social Council on human rights issues. The next step will be to work cooperatively with the UN body to report human rights abuses in Ethiopia.

The Australian group is the only Oromia support group in the world to receive this status. They believe this will help others who work on the same issues, such as Ogaden and Sudema.

Oromia is part of the Unrepresented Nations and Peoples' Or-ganisation, represented by the Oromo Liberation front (OLF). In 2007, there were approximately 31 million Oromo people. They speak some dialects and mainly Oromiffa. Their religions are Christianity, Islam and Traditional religion. Main tribes are Barona and Barento.

An account of the struggle of the Oromo people to affirm their place in History, involves the fact that they are so numerous in Ethiopia and yet have recently been subjected to violence and some say, genocide. They make up a significant portion of the Horn of Africa population. Their sufferings are not well known.

## Population

It has one of the most numerous in Africa. At least 20 million people speak Oromo as their first language. Oromians make up about 40% of the population of Ethiopia. Apart from a small number of pastoralists who live in Kenya, all their homelands lie in Ethiopia.

*Celebrating a religious festival*

## Economy

Agriculture is the main occupation, with around 90% of the peo-ple involved. As well as Coffee and Khat, they work with hides, skins, pulses, oil. There are gold mines, platinum, salt, sulpher, iron-ore, gas. Hot springs are developing into a rich source of tourist dollars. The rivers and springs could also generate electric pow-er. Farmers still use wooden ploughs, pulled by oxen.

## Political Groups

Because the Oromarians want their home country to be its own sovereign State, they are working hard to get United Nations approval. Matters move very slowly.

One very successful lobby group is the Oromia Support Group Australia who worked really hard to attend the UN's group for Economic and Social Council and report how things are going in Africa.

The Oromarians also belong to the Unrepresented Nations and Peoples' Organisation (UNPO) and the Oromo Liberation Front (OLF).

The UNPO is a political organisation established in 1973, by Oromo nationalists. They aimed to lead the people against the Abyssinian colonization. They are called the Oromo Liberation Front (OLF). This was formed because the people wanted its Statehood to be recognized again.

The OLF wants a political union with other nations as equals. They strongly believe that their quest for self-determination is just and legitimate. They believe it is in line with the principle enshrined in the Charter of the UN.

In 1991, a Tigrean regime took over form the Amhara rulers, but is seen by the people of Oromia to just be a cosmetic change, doing nothing for the Oromarians.

The OLF and Oromo people want a union of free people. The OLF joined the UNPO in 2004.

There is an Oromo Democratic Party and an Oromo Federalist Democratic Movement, which in May 2005, won 11 seats all form the Oromo region and the Oromo People's Congress. This last is a major opposition political party in Ethiopia.

# People

Between the 12th and 15th centuries the Oromo had separated into 2 major groups of tribes: the Borana and the Barentu and several minor groups. The Barentu moved to the eastern regions. The Borana people moved into other areas. They live in southern Ethiopia (Oromia) and speak a dialect of Oromo. They are know especially for their historic Gadaa political system and they follow traditional religions, Christianity, Islam and traditional.

They remain pagan and worship a "Sky God". Their society of men are divided into age-set groups. They remain in these groups all their lives. This is similar to the Dinka groups in South Sudan, but is a much stronger system. In the north, the Oromo are Muslim or members of the Ethiopian Orthodox Tewahedo Church through acculturation.

Fourteen groups have Oromo in their names: Borana Oromo people, Guii Oromo people, Welega Oromo people and Harerge Oromo people. They speak Eastern Oromo language and Southern Oromo language.

## Gadaa

The Borana and other Oromo communities governed them-selves with Gadaa. This was a "limited democratic socio-political system" before the 16th century. The Gadaa system saw men elected leaders for 8 year terms. .roles.

The men came from five Oromo groups. They carried out judicial, political, ritual and religious .Each major clan followed this sys-tem of self government.

Women and people from the lower Oromo castes were exclud-ed. Men born in the upper Oromo castes undertook their 8 years as their lives became established their role and status.

As well, every 8 years, by consensus, an Abbaa Bokkuu was elected, responsible for justice, peace, judicial and ritual pro-cesses. The highest strata were Borana Oromo and the lowest were slaves.

## Oromo People in Australia

The Oromo community is one of the emergingcommunities and in Australia, its numbers are estimated to be greater than 10,000. In 2014 the number was estimated to be fewer than 3,000. The majority live in Melbourne. In Ethiopia, they are estimated at 40 million people, making them close to being 50% of Ethiopians.

Oromo people have settled peacefully in Australia since the 1980s. They prefer to be called Australian Oromo. They speak Oromo which helps them retain their sense of identity.

## Community Life

Most Oromo who have come to Australia, have spent time in a refugee camp. This forced flight to a refugee camp, brings its own traumas. Life is very harsh and single mothers find it very difficult to care for their children.

Coming to Melbourne, they find about 5,000 other Oromo and can start building friendships easily. Their main focus is strongly to learn English and have their children attend school and do their best.

They also need to be educated, and this is the most important thing for Oromo women. Women need extra help with health and welfare issues. For example, in Oromo, children were taught respect for their elders. They learnt by a combination of family pressure and the occasional smack. Fear of the Child Protection Service, can lead to a fear of correcting their child's behaviour. Plus children can learn form Australian families, their United Nations Rights and tell their parents about that rule.

Oromo people, like all people love to come together and dance, talk, sing and enjoy being together. They are a peaceful group of new Australians.

African-Australian Multicultural Employment and Youth Services (AAMEYS)
Suite 108, Level 1, 144-148 Nicholson St, Footscray, Vic, 3011
03-9042 1604 or 0405 479 275
Email: info@aameys.com.au or harmony@aameys.com.au.
Website: www.aameys.com.au
Facebook: https://www.facebook.com/aameys/
LinkedIn: https://au.linkedin.com/company/aameysofficial

Donations: Please donate to BSB No. 633000; Account # 1507 50149, for further info contact Dr Berhan Ahmed on 0405479275 or 03 9042 1604.

## References

Diasporaaction.org.au/Oromia-support-group-Australia-o/
https://advocacy4oromia.org/home/oromoin-victoria
https://www.ukessays.com/essays/history/
https://www.youtube.com/channel//bwPosFpYK6hPUQteOf7fYg
https://www.goodreads.com/book/show/2820714-oromia
https://www.facebook.com/oromia430/
https://oassociationv.wordpress.com/about—oava/
https://issafrica.s3.amazonaws.com/site/uploads/mono-202-2.pdf
https://oromia.today
https://oromiamedia.com
https://www.britannica.com/topic/Oromo
https://unpo.org/members/7917
Www.oromoliberationfront.org/OromiaBriefs.htm

# Somalia

*Independence Day July 1st*

*Shoppers in Hamarwayne market in Mogadishu*

## Map of Somalia

Somalia is a country with one of its borders being the Indian Ocean. It is bounded by Kenya, Ethiopia and Eritrea. It is estimated to have 15 million citizens. Its capital city is Mogadishu in the south of the country.

There are currently 6 States, although their borders are still a matter for argument. In this map, the pink and red States are called Somaliland, yellow is Puntland, green is Hirshabelle, orange is South West State and blue is Jubaland.

Somalia has the longest coastline in Africa.

The population is around 15 million, 43% of the population lives on less than US1 per day. Money is made by livestock, remittances from the Diaspora is a second largest earner, and telecommunications is the third.

## Somalian Political History

## A brief overview of major events

Muslim Arabs and Persians established trading posts along Somalia's coasts from the 7li1 to 10li1 century. Somalian warriors joined Muslim sultanates in their battles with Christian Ethiopia in the 15th and 16th centuries. Britain, France and Italy began to dominate the region in the 19th century. Britain established a protectorate in 1887 and concluded an agreement with France in 1888 defining their Somalian possessions. Italy created a small protectorate in 1889 and added territory in the south. Somali speaking districts of Ethiopia were combined with Italian Somaliland in 1936 to form Italian east Africa. Britain conquered Italian Somaliland in World War 11, and renamed Somalia, it gained internal autonomy in 1956 and independence and unification with British Somaliland in 1960.

In 1969 a coup led by major general Muhammad Siyad Barre resulted in a socialist state. In 1977 the corrupt and repressive regime broke with the USSR over Soviet aid to Ethiopia and received aid during the 1980s from the US. The Somali army invaded the Ogaden region in 1977 but was defeated by the Ethiopians.

In Mogadishu and most of the south the United Somali Congress achieved control, but savage warfare erupted between rival subclans. Almost a quarter of the population faced starvation because of the fighting. UN food supplies and peacekeepers arrived in 1992 and were soon joined by troops from the US and other nations to assure distribution of food aid.

A national cease-fire was signed, but no central government formed. Fighting again erupted (1993) in Mogadishu as the UN unsuccessfully attempted to arrest gen.

Mohammed Farah Aidid. The US and other nations withdrew their forces in 1994 and the last UN forces were withdrawn in 1995. That year some factions declared Aidid president, but the rest of the country remained divided into spheres of influence, with no central government. Aidid died from battle wounds in 1996, and his faction chose his son, to succeed him.

The country was devastated by floods in 1997, and in the late 1990s was still without an organized, internationally recognized government. Breakaway states were declared in Puntland (NE) and Jubaland (S) in 1998. In 2000 a Somali conference in Djibouti established a national charter and elected a 225 national assembly and a president, Abdikassim Salad Hassan. Salad returned to Somalia in August, but several militias refused to recognize the new government, which has little real authority. Somaliland voted (2001) to remain independent, and in 2002 warlords in SW Somalia formed another breakaway government in Baidoa.

A cease-fire accord (October '2002) among all major factions except Somaliland failed to halt all fighting, and subsequent talks failed to produce significant results. Meanwhile, the mandate of the essentially symbolic interim government expired in August 2003, but the president withdrew from talks, refused to resign, and had the prime minister (who remained in the talks) removed from office.

In September 2004, after many delays, a 275-member parliament was convened in Kenya under the new charter, and a new president, Abdullahi Yusuf Ahmed, was elected in October. Yusuf, a former general who had served as president of Puntland, and the parliament are to serve for 5 years. Somaliland remained a nonparticipant in the transitional government.

## Brief History

In antiquity, Somalia was an important commercial centre. By the Middle Ages, several powerful empires dominated regional trade. In the late 19th century British and Italian empires established colonies.

In 1977 a corrupt and repressive regime broke with the USSR over Soviet aid to Ethiopia and received aid for the USA. The Somali Army invaded the Ogaden region in 1977 but was defeated by the Ethiopians.

In 1991 Somali civil war broke out. Most regions returned to customary and religious war.

In Mogadishu savage warfare erupted between rival subclans. Almost a quarter of the population faced starvation. UN food supplies and peacekeepers arrived in 1992.

A national ceasefire was signed, but no central government was formed. The USA withdrew its forces along with the other nations in 1994 and the UN withdrew in 1995. That year some factions declared Aidid President, but the rest of the country remained divided. He died in 1996. His son was elected.

The country was devastated by floods in 1997, and in the 1990s was still without an organized, internationally recognized government. Breakaway States were declared in Puntland and Jubaland in 1998.

A ceasefire accord 2002 was among all major factions, except Somaliland. They failed to cease all fighting.

In 2004 the Transitional Federal Government reestablished the military. Somaliland stayed out.

In 2012 a new provisional constitution was passed confirming Somalia as a federation.

## 2019, 23rd October

High-Level UN-AU Delegation Highlight Somalia's Progress and

Challenges with Women in women's participation in its peace, security and development efforts– while also calling for further progress. "Amidst the ongoing violence the people of Somalia still faces, the country has made enormous strides on its path to peace and stability" (UN Press Statement, 2019)

The aim of the one-day visit was to express the UN and African Union's commitment to work with the Somali people in their pursuit of peace, stability and credible elections. The delegation underscored the importance of women's meaningful participation in political, peace and security efforts, particularly in relation to countering violent extremism, holding elections and advancing development efforts.

Progress towards peace is incredibly slow and will continue to be a huge matter for concern. While factions are still fighting, the country cannot provide a safe, heathy place for its citizens.

# Religion

The vast majority – 99%, are Sunni Muslims and it is the clans which are not stopping fighting.

# Religion and health issues
From: www.islam-usa.com/e40.html

- Cleanliness is considered "half of the faith". Qur'an, the holy book, prohibits eating pork or pork products, meat of dead animals, blood and all intoxicants.
- Respect a Muslim's modesty and privacy. Some health examinations can be done over a gown. Provide same sex health care persons, if possible. Always examine a female patient in the presence of another female.
- Some Muslim men will not shake a woman's hand.

- Provide Muslim or Kosher meals.
- Allow them to pray, and if they can read, to read the Qur'an.
- Take time to explain medical tests, procedures and treatment.
- During a birthing, it is preferred that the father be the sole male present.

There is also a range of deep cultural beliefs and attitudes in Muslim communities towards disability that need to be discussed. They are:

- A social stigma with corresponding fear of "visibility" in the community.
- A curse or punishment for some wrongdoing. This belief is evident among other cultures, such as north Sudanese.
- A gift from God or God-given, when a disadvantaged child or person is seen as a blessing.

## Christian and Muslim families

Family is the foundation of Somalian society. The peace and security offered by a stable family unit is greatly valued and is seen as essential for the spiritual growth of its members. A harmonious social order is created by the existence of extended families. Children are treasured, and rarely leave home until they marry.

## Christians, Muslims and the Elderly

In Somalia there are no old peoples' homes. The practice of caring for one's elderly relatives is considered an honour and blessing, and an opportunity for great spiritual growth. God asks that we pray for our parents, but act with limitless compassion, remembering that when we were helpless little children, they preferred to help us rather than themselves.

Mothers are particularly respected in both religions. The Prophet Mohammed said "Paradise lies at the feet of mothers".

When they reach old age, Somalian parents are treated mercifully, with kindness and selflessness. Serving one's parents is a duty second only to prayer, and it is their right to expect it. It is considered despicable to express any irritation, if an old person becomes difficult.

Respite care and nursing homes may be used. Hospitals are also acceptable to many, however people without English are frightened about remaining in mainstream institutions.

## Communication of diagnosis/prognosis in a medical situation

News of an illness is first given to the family – the closest member to the patient. The next of kin will advise the immediate family, but perhaps advice will not be given to friends.

Patients are often not told about a life-threatening disease, as it is felt that to do so might make their condition worse. They also may be ostracized by their community because people may consider them infectious and/or cursed.

Every family is different. Plus, after being in a western country for several years, the understanding of English could be fairly good, so it might be possible to tell the person gently about the diagnosis. If a patient wants to know, tell him/her.

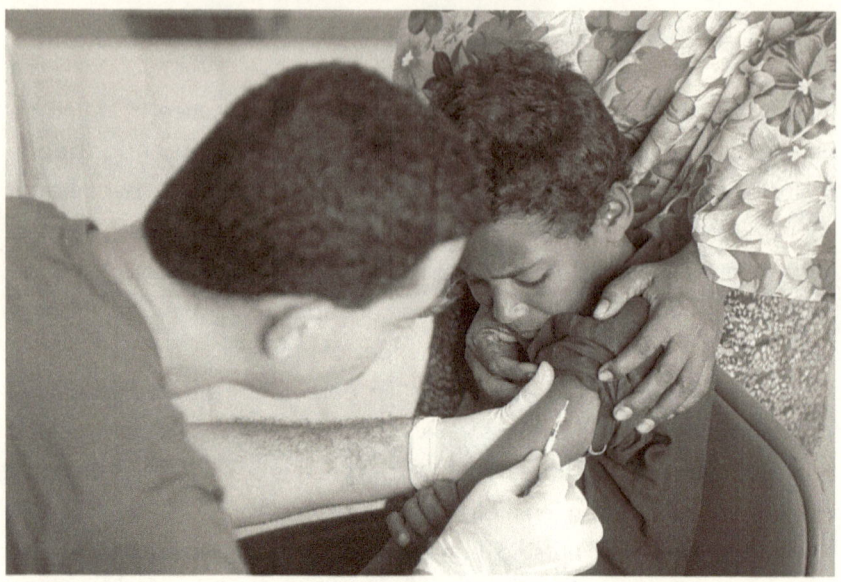

In some cases, the family leaves all the telling to the medical staff, in other families, the wisest person will manage the telling.

Words like "dying" and "cancer" are used with sensitivity, as for any group. Cancer is sometimes referred to as "That Disease". Avoid discussing death, dying and how long a person is likely to live.

When a person is dying, family and friends are called in to stay until the person passes away. The Qur'an is recited until they pass away. Once the person has died, the house is open, and condolences are received. There are no celebrations or frivolities. Burial and religious rites are performed within 24 hours.

## Role and acceptable behaviours of health professionals/volunteers

It would be preferable if the treating professionals are the same gender as the patient. Some men will not shake hands with a woman.

Many families remove their shoes at the door.

Visitors to a Muslim home should be aware that alcoholic drinks are not permitted. Pig in any form is forbidden. Meat must be Halal – slaughtered in a special way with prayers being said.

Health professionals should be aware that Muslims wash and then pray five times a day.

All pain relief is allowed.

Information provision is helpful, and the language of the family members must be considered. Many refugees speak 4 or sometimes more, languages and English may not be their main language.

Other ways of sharing information is to call a meeting, run a forum, hold a discussion seminar, use the language of the people being worked with.

## Ethnic groups

Somali 85%, Bantu and other non-Somali 15% (including Arabs 30,000)

## Life Expectancy

Total population: 48.09 years
Male: 46.36 years
Female: 49.87 years
Age structure: 0 – 14 years 44.5%
15 – 64years 52.9%
65 and over 2.6%

It is clear to see the effects of war, poor nutrition, a lack of medical services has a clear negative effect on the population.

## Major infectious diseases

There is a very high risk of developing an infectious disease. There are food or waterborne diseases, bacterial and protozoal diarrhea, hepatitis and Typhoid fever. As well there are Vector borne diseases: malaria, and dengue fever are high risks in some locations. Water contact disease: schistosomiasis. Animal contact disease: rabies (2004 lists of disease).

## Somalian Families and Traditions, Somalian Clans

Ethnic Somalis are united by language, culture, devotion to Islam and to a common ancestor, the Samaale or Samaal. Genealogical ties trace their genealogical origin to the mythical founding father. Genealogy constitutes the heart of the Somali social system.

Although between one and three million Somalis live in the Diaspora, they still know their place within the traditional clan system, so they can be easily identified according to their clan, sub-clan, sub-sub-clan and so on.

The major branches of the Somali lineage system are 4 overwhelmingly pastoral, nomadic clan families. (The Dir, Daarood, Isaaq, and Hawiye, who are collectively denoted by the appellation of Samaal) and the 2 agricultural ones (the Digil and Rahanwayn). These clans are prone to internal schism and factionalism. Most Somalis tend to give greater emotional and political power to their lineages. Clans have become more powerful as a result of all the political upheaval.

The Dir, Darood, Isaaq and Hawiye constitute roughly 75% of the population. These people are widely distributed pastoralists or settled cultivators. The Digil and Rahanwayn constitute about 25% of the population and are settled in the south of the country. They rely on a mixed economy of cattle and camel husbandry and cultivation.

The traditional social structure was characterized by competition and conflict between descent groups. Clans fought each other over pasture, water, trade, religious matters and encroachments of camel herding nomads.

To varying degrees, the pole of power in the politics of independent Somalia generally have tended to form around the Daarwood clanfamily and a confederacy of the Hawiye and Isaaq clanfamilies.

This system of clanfamilies lacks a concept of individual culpability. When a man commits homicide, for example, the guilt does not remain with him solely as an individual murderer as in most western societies; the crime is attributed to all of the murderer's kin, who become guilty. Members of the aggrieved group then seek revenge, on any member of the clanfamily they meet.

As well, this system is vulnerable to manipulation, for example, the head of state such as Siad Barre, who used the resources of the state to reward and punish entire clans collectively. He did this to take attention away from his increasingly unpopular regime.

## General information

Family size: In Australia, Somali families have an average of 6 or more children. Many families have more than this. The family is led by the husband and he is in charge of most aspects of the family's life. This has made the lives of many Australian Somalis very difficult because so many of them arrived without their husband, due to all the wars and violence.

Migration waves: Somali settlement began in the 1990s. Many entrants were young men, although recently a large number of young mothers have arrived with young children. Most are women whose husbands have died in the wars.

Language: The official language is Somali. Some arrivals speak English and some Italian. Oral language is very important as the Somali language began to be written in 1975. Spelling often varies for place names and cities.

## Traditional family structure

A traditional family might consist of a mother and father, 4-8 children. A nuclear family consists of grandparents, aunts, uncles and other relatives.

Generally, the family is patriarchal in which the father is the main provider and the woman is the general manager of the family's domestic affairs. Women are regarded as the equal of a man, but the man has the final voice in a decision. Increasingly women are playing a role in helping provide for the family, especially as the wars keep killing men more than women. In Australia mothers often come without their husband, due to war.

Women are highly regarded in Islamic law. Women and men are under the same obligations and rules of conduct. Differences emerge when it comes to pregnancy, childbirth and clothing.

The Quran requires Muslim women to dress modestly and the same applies to men. The Prophet Mohammed's wives were required to were total covering, but it is not a command that all women cover themselves totally. It is a matter of practice and differs from country to country. Almost universal is the hijab, the head scarf.

There is not a tradition of physical violence, because the Islamic religion prevents men from physically hitting a woman. A man is only permitted to hit his wife if all avenues of discussion, separation, and appeals to the elders have failed. A man may divorce his wife but a woman does not have that right. If she leaves her husband, elders will counsel her against this. If she is still determined to stay away, the elders talk with the husband and advise him to divorce hr. A woman's salary and dowry are hers to keep.

## Settlement Issues in Australia

**Housing:** there is a difficulty providing government housing for the large families. Private rental is expensive and difficult to get because they have no previous record of good tenancy.

**Money issues:** Somalian refugees send so much of their Centrelink money back to Somalia; it makes up 23% of Somalia's GDP. This adds to the pressure for Somali families in Australia where you have to buy everything and pay bills.

Women receive money from Centrelink, and they are good money managers. They gain confidence budgeting their income. They are also successful business people. Older children also receive money and become skilled at saving to buy new things they want, like mobile phones.

It takes the men a little time to become used to their wife having her own money. Some marriages do not survive the situation.

**Changing family roles:** lack of role models, particularly male, for youths has led to attitude and behavioral problems. Men finding it difficult to secure employment and become frustrated and humiliated, as men are the providers in Somalia. Many younger women have come to Australia without their husbands, who may be killed or fighting somewhere.

Mothers are the Heads of the Family, which is new. They are responsible for all aspects of a family's life and this is very stressful. Women find each day to be really busy. They attend English classes, locate childcare, take children to and from school, learn about the expectations that schools have of parents, and manage children who are also struggling to get used to a new country.

One of the largest sources of stress is the behaviour of Youths. Their behaviour runs contrary to traditional Somali behaviour, which is family centred and respectful of elders. Youths are caught between 2 cultures and can be unsure of their place in either culture. Traditional ways can seem "old fashioned" and "inappropriate to life in Australia.

Somali mothers are keen to learn new skills, especially of parenting. They also want to learn about the Australian laws and culture. If a family arrives with both parents, there are marriage breakdowns, which would not happen so much in Somalia. A woman has different rights than she'd have in Somalia. These change the relationship between the parents. Social security money gives a woman new independence. Family violence can occur, for many reasons such as stress, frustrations or misunderstandings of the role change which occurs for women.

**Family separation:** causes feelings of grief and loneliness among families. Separation also increases pressure on families as there is no extended family to look after children in Australia.

**Inter-generational conflict:** particularly between youth and the elderly as the young generation are adapting to an Australian lifestyle, often rejecting their Somali culture.

**Racism:** the Somali communities believe that racist attitudes can affect them with employment, housing and other opportunities.

**Emotional wellbeing: mental health:** it is felt by Somalis, that this is their area of greatest health problems. Depression, anxiety, Post Traumatic Stress Disorder is an increasing problem due to torture, trauma which has been experienced by every refugee, added to these diseases is culture shock and pressures of settling in Australia.

**Physical disability:** due to strict laws regarding the health of refugees who are accepted into Australia, there is not a high incidence of physically disabled Somalians here. There will be some war injuries, but mostly these Somalians have gone to Belgium.

**Literacy and language:** It is important to be aware that there maybe literacy issues with new arrivals. The use of Interpreters is highly valued and makes a service provider's life easier, if the information is understood quickly.

## Nutrition for women

In Australia, refugees maintained their diet of the country of their birth. They can increase consumption of some processed foods, such as instant noodles, crisps and pizza. However, there is little evidence that the families eat a lot of prepared meals or takeaways. A significant addition

*The Port of Bosaso harbor.*

to their diet was the use of breakfast cereals. Substitution of ready made bread over traditional bread and lamb instead of camel is clear.

Women and men are becoming overweight, as a result of a lack of exercise, plus some take away foods. Children have a growing problem with their teeth rotting. This needs community education. It is important to encourage people to maintain their traditional diet, while adopting healthy foods from the host country.

Muslim attitudes to Religion and Health, and old age have a wide range of attitudes, responses and experiences with disability: Factors such as level of education, access to medical information, and rural or urban upbringing are important.

REFERENCES
Beckwith C and Fischer A, "African Ceremonies", Harry N. Abrams Inc, New York, 2002
Community Referral Directory, Pty.Ltd., Emerald, Victoria
Dept. NSW Multicultural Health Communication Service website
https://mhcs.health.nsw.gov.au. "Domestic Violence Hurts The Whole Family", 1998.Somali language.
Dick, Bob. Action Research Resources, Southern Cross University, Australia
Gardiner, E Osman, A. 2005. "Somalia Culture, Disability and Aging in the Somalian Community". Action on Disability in Ethnic Communities, Australia.
Internet: www.somaliheritage.com
www.islamforchristians.com/islam-social-behavior

# South Sudan

*Independence Day July 4th*

The World's Newest Country

Juba, the capital of South Sudan, on the banks of the River Nile.

# South Sudanese Australians

## The South Sudanese Family in South Sudan

Traditional South Sudanese families are, by Australian norms, large. There can be 5 or 6 children commonly. They are multi-generational grouped by clear bloodlines or by marriage, languages, songs and oral history. They all live and sleep together, so when a family member is away, marries or leaves for a western country, they are very much missed by those who stay behind.

It is extremely difficult for those who leave to explain to those who stay, information about their new lives in a new country. The question of sending money back to South Sudan causes much resentment, confusion and stress. Everyone tries to send some money back, and the amounts vary, according to whether the former refugee has paid employment or not.

Life in a village is difficult, as there is not modern infrastructure, so roads are often just tracks worn down by the feet of the villagers. There are also few medical services available. Babies are born in the village, without medical assistance. Skilled traditional midwives are present.

Regarding education, there is a mixture of modern sheds and buildings used but the vast majority of schools is a local village setting, with a blackboard placed under a tree. Children mainly sit in the dirt and make their marks in the soil. There are a few large-scale schools, such as the Loreto school at Rumbek, run by Loreto nuns.

This school educates boys and girls at Primary levels and then girls can continue until Year 12. The school says they want to educate women to use all their skills and abilities. There are over 1000 students. It is supported by an international, large group of other Loreto graduates. This school is an exception. There is a small number of governments run schools, no teacher training and no genuine Education Policy being activated in South Sudan. The majority of citizens, especially women are illiterate.

Some villages only have 1 public water source, using bore water. Traditional houses do not have bathrooms, toilets, electricity. Women grow crops for food and meat is scarce.

## The role of Cows

Rural families have their wealth in cattle. Sudanese cattle are much loved by the people. Young men have their own favourite cow, bull or ox and spend days composing songs and poems to their favourite. Cattle are not usually slaughtered for food, but for a special occasion like when a guest has travelled a long way or there is a marriage or death. Milk is an important part of the diet, and village women keep sheep and goats for this purpose. When an animal is slaughtered, all of it is used.

Even city based South Sudanese value cows highly and maintain contact with their rural cousins. Cattle come in a large range of colours and spots and learn to know their owner well. The Dinka have a Dowry tradition of a groom paying a girl's family for her hand in Marriage. The price of this Dowry was always paid in cows. A larger number would be paid for a young girl with an impeccable lineage, who is quiet, well behaved and follows traditional ways. In Australia, there has been a change and now cash is used to seal the transaction between two families. The amounts differ according to qualities, education level, looks, nature of the girl. The amount can be thousands of dollars. These days, if a young woman has academic qualifications, the amount of the dowry can be tens of thousands of dollars. It causes the groom's family a lot of difficulty paying.

There are young women who brought 200 cows through Dowry payment to her father and male relatives and there are happy women who are worth 20 cows. There is a process undertaken to decide the size of the Dowry. It can take a few days to decide but in Australia it can be decided in one day or over a weekend. The process begins to be formally recognized when the two families sit together to discuss how much the

groom's family will have to pay. In Australia, a Hall is often used, and people share a meal after the bargaining.

The two families sit opposite the other, there are main negotiators, with a support team and the rest of the male family group sits behind them. In the middle there is an Agelong, a man who calls out the discussion and negotiation, so that everyone can hear what is going on.

Negotiations are long and not always smoothly conducted. Eventually, a decision is made and a deal arrived at. Sometimes this step is called "the marriage', because this is where the decision to marry a young man to a woman is decided.

The marriage is these days, a traditional western style service and Reception, not an African service.

Tribal conflict is common in South Sudan and can be devastating. The two largest tribes – the Dinka and the Nuer have a long history of mistrust and battles. There are 64 tribes in South Sudan, some have more than 1 million people and others are small, but all of them keep their traditions going and will fight if there is a problem. Men battle using shields of cow hide and long shaped sticks. Women also sometimes will fight. There is a saying that in a battle, a man can hurt you, but if a woman strikes you,

you will probably die. They are fierce fighters and fight for their families. Currently in South Sudan, there are small inter-tribal wars continuing. (Sudan Tribune 2016).

In the past 100 years more than half the years have been spent fighting various wars. Therefore, citizens are very experienced in fighting but when it comes to peace, there is not the same level of knowing how to maintain peace. Peace is doomed to failure until the country's leadership is also at peace, one tribe with another. There is a great need for people to learn how to make peace, both in Australia and in South Sudan. Peace can be taught.

Life is always lived with the threat of a new war erupting. The climate is often one of drought and there is always the threat of dangers. Schools are scarce, medical services are few, the Court system is also lacking in processes and legal staff. South Sudan has a long way to go before it is westernized or has modern infrastructure developed.

The shock of coming to a western democracy is immense. One man spoke for some others when he said, "We thought we would be able to live our traditional lives in Australia. We never knew we would have to give up so much of our culture". For Australians, and new Australians, they should have been properly taught even for a short amount of time, about life in Australia. Our capital cities are very large and there is no-way that people could keep their cows close to their homes. The whole adjustment of people is like a massive jump forward in time for the South Sudanese.

# Contemporary families in Australia and South Sudan

In Australia, life changes drastically from a life of living according to the rhythms of nature and war. The first part of becoming a refugee is when a family group – mother, father, children and sometimes one of the adult's parents leave their village or house in a town and travel as best they can,

to a large Refugee Camp or just arrive in a neighbouring country, such as Kenya.

Travel is very difficult and dangerous and takes a long time. Some refugees are lucky and they can catch a train or bus, but that all costs money which many people do not have. Living in a refugee camp can be really dangerous. People are desperate and fight, there's a lack of food, and a small amount of medical assistance is available. On the positive side, some refugees get work through the service agencies located in the camps. And most refugees can receive some care and food from international organisations. The interaction with international workers brings dividends around the refugee such as maybe learning some English. At the least, those who do interact with workers can gain an understanding of the different way of life of westerners. When they travel to a western country, this knowledge is helpful.

Life in Australia is all new and confusing, and people say everything is difficult, not just the language. Money becomes increasingly important. In South Sudan, villagers have animals and home-grown vegetables to eat. In Australia you need to find out about where to go to get food and clothing. You must quickly learn about having a bank account and learn to carefully manage the Centrelink money. Shopping in a Supermarket is also new and very challenging.

People usually shop in South Sudan at the same places for many years, as their food consumption is not new. Women buy the same ingredients and tend to cook traditional meals. Relatives or their Sponsor takes them through each of these challenges in Australia and everyone learns gradually.

Education is another big learning curve. Some South Sudanese have learned the English alphabet at a village school. This is a school held in the shade of a huge tree in the village. Students sit on the ground and may write in the dust. In Australia, children attend a Special English Language school, adults can attend Adult Migrant English Service (AMES) and they receive 500 free hours of tuition.

Owning a television helps people learn English, along with reading every bit of English they can, via "junk mail" or newspapers.

## Modern South Sudanese families in Australia

South Sudanese former refugees are similar to other groups of former refugees. Everyone needs to learn to speak English. They do that via AMES and 500 hours of free tuition or by watching television, or by reading local newspapers or by eventually going online. It takes years to be fluent. Children learn faster and more accurately than adults.

Another new experience is that all family members are busy outside the house, with the only exceptions being the Elders. Elders tend to stay at home, where they can be useful by taking children to school and bringing them home again. The women can also cook for the family.

Male Elders do very little to help the family in a direct sense. They don't mind children, clean or cook. Some might do some shopping, but usually male Elders sit in cafes and chat. They talk about people who are having a good time of settling and those who are suffering. They gossip, sharing these stories. Female Elders often have care of the little children after school or going to or coming from childcare, so their lives become shaped by this. They do not sit in cafes gossiping but can meet at another lady's home to chat. Some drive their own cars which is a huge change in their lives.

One of the most significant challenges in Australia is that all members of the family have to daily leave their house to get into education or work. All adults receive some money through Centrelink. Even Elders are expected to look for work, which is unheard of in South Sudan where Elders are treated very kindly by their families. This is just one example of how Australia shows its lack of understanding about the South Sudanese people: its new arrivals. Many Elders cannot read or write in their own language, let alone know enough English to get and keep a job. Women are more likely to be illiterate when compared with their husbands. Most South Sudanese languages have not been written. Dinka was only recorded after the 1940s.

Africa World Books (AWB) was established in 2013, to address these very issues. It works hard to encourage writing one's story and publishing the stories. AWB believes that it is important for the history and myths and legends to be written down and kept for the future. Elders are ageing and people are dying without recording their stories. AWB is working hard to record the histories.

The 510 hours at AMES is often not taught in a way that is understandable to the new arrivals. It would help people learn if there was an Interpreter available to co-teach.

Children learn English fast and can become Interpreters for their parents. This can cause problems because the new concepts, ideas, requirements are all very strange and children cannot easily understand the terms used. The same problem exists when an adult goes to see a doctor. If the children interpret, sometimes the wrong information is given by the child. The increased use of Interpreters should be mandated.

Elders and adults all try to save money for a car and driving lessons. Public transport is also used, but takes time and shopping or collecting all the children from school is quite difficult to do using public transport. Families are very proud of their cars and keep them spotless.

Getting a license comes after someone has taught the adults and Elders how to drive. Initially, South Sudanese former refugees used to believe that a Learner's Permit was a license to drive legally and that belief took a couple of years to stop. Again, why weren't they told? Road rules are also hard to learn, as driving in South Sudan follows rules in the cities but not in rural areas. Some people will have learnt the city's ways and others will start from scratch. Men expect to get a car and license, but not women. In Australia, women save money, pay for lessons and have bought themselves a car. This is a revolutionary step in female emancipation, as are their education opportunities.

Children go to Childcare, Primary or Secondary schools. They are quick to learn but get very little help from home, unless their parents are literate and see the value of education. If they are, then children's schoolwork is treated as important. Today, many children are completing Year 12, with many continuing their education at a Tertiary level. There is also a large group of Master's degree holders and also Doctorates of Philosophy. This is a source of joy for the people becoming qualified.

# Refugees from South Sudan and the Uniting Nations role

All South Sudanese refugees have been investigated by a United Nations process. All their family history is taken down and must be shown to be truthful. It is vey detailed. Aspiring refugees must pass this test. South Sudanese refugees do not try to come by boat, despite what the Liberal

Party claimed. They arrive fully vetted, by air. They have proved to the UN that they are genuine refugees, in danger in their own country.

South Sudanese refugees have been coming to Australia since the early 2000s. A few came in the later 1990s. In 2003 and 2004/5 they were the largest number of refugees arriving under the United Nations Humanitarian system. South Sudanese came to be 54% of the total intake in 2003/4 and the following year were 63.6% of all Humanitarian refugees. They were the largest group to come in those years. In 2004/5, their numbers were about 4 times the size of the next group, the Iraqi and ten times more than the next African group, the Liberians.

South Sudan is still finding its way in a modern world. The Government moves extremely slowly to introduce programs and services to benefit citizens. Infrastructure remains poor, especially in the much-needed areas of education and medicine. If a person is rich and living in a town, then they usually afford to fly to another country for medical tests and operations.

The Government Ministers are not elected but appointed by the President Salva Kiir Mayardit. Less than 10 years ago, a few Ministers were not even literate. It is thought there has been an improvement in the calibre of men chosen to lead. Women are still mainly excluded by the regime. People did not elect Salva Kiir. He was the First Vice President to Dr. John Garang who was killed in a helicopter crash. The first Vice President these days is a Nuer man, Riek Machar. The animosity and fear from each man holds up much development. The second Vice President is a Dinka. So, it is clear that unless these three men can work together peacefully, the unstable, often aggressive Government will be hampered in pursuing peace. Meanwhile, the citizens are forced to live often in continual fear that the Army will attack them in their village and take hostages and food.

South Sudanese middle aged and older people suffer the most in Australia. These days, most of the former refugees can speak enough English to live with and work. Many have jobs, many more have entered tertiary education and are very successful. The new Australians are proving to be intelligent, capable and resilient.

The refugees have to make a lot of "jumps" in their thinking, to learn about life in Australia. As they travelled to Australia, it has been like they have travelled in time. Their home experiences no longer help them live good lives here. Daily routines and activities all come from the 21st Century. Things most of us take for granted are new and need to be understood. Can you imagine finding the following new, and strange? Electricity, television, Smart phones, driving a car, using a shower or flush toilet, running clean water for taps all the time, getting bills for services such as water usage, catching public transport, budgeting, shopping in Supermarkets, doctor's visits, health treatments: everything needs to be explained and understood.

The refugees know very little about these things at first and they can be extremely strange and even frightening for them.

# Family Issues and Challenges

One of the areas where change impacts heavily, is in the area of relationships between men and women. In South Sudan, a man is head of the family and may have many wives. A woman can get a divorce, but it takes time and a lot of talking and listening has to be undertaken before one is granted. Cruelty and failure to provide are two grounds on which a divorce can be given. The process involves most of the adults in the man's family and the woman's parents. If a divorce is given, all the Dowry money or cows must be returned to the groom's family, so divorce is still rare.

Men are thought to be superior to women. In a traditional family, a wife has the same status as a young boy and there are ways of behaving that look strange to a western way of thinking. In his book, *The Dinka History* by Lewis Anei Madut-Kuendit, he writes that in marriage a man may

"... reserve the right to reprimand and even beat their wives as a means to discipline them and make them behave and comply with the wishes and rules of the family and the husband in the home". (Madut-Kuendit, 2016). If she "has to be persistently beaten and habitually insulted for no good cause, her relatives may agree to a divorce". (Ibid).

Australia's divorce laws were drastically changed in the 1970s, to recognize no-fault divorce. In the past, divorce was difficult to get and really expensive. There were several reasons for getting a divorce, for example Adultery was one ground on which to ask for a divorce. It was a complicated process in which the man generally agreed to be found in the arms of a lady, not his wife. When this was referred to in court, it was the end of his marriage and husband and wife went home happily. No fault divorce made the divorce very simple and quick. This new form sped up court cases and made women the legal equals of men in a marriage. South Sudanese men have been very genuinely shocked at the large number of divorces and separations that have occurred among their friends here. Women quickly realized that the Australian courts could be used to extricate them from a marriage. They knew that Police are mandated to attend a home if a person rang and said a beating was occurring. Women learned that this was step one in what they call, "gaining their freedom". Some were reporting the truth of their situation and some just used the rules to oust a man they almost no longer needed.

Men have been slowly facing facts that this is an Australian Family Law rule and they must accept it. Getting an Intervention Order to prevent a husband returning to the marital home, has also had a massive effect on South Sudanese men. At first, they didn't know about Intervention Orders, then some refused to follow the rulings and now, some try to win their wives back with genuine remorse and a change of behaviours. But a large percentage of South Sudanese former wives have failed to accept the man's return. And the number of men who have gone back to live in South Sudan is possibly over one hundred from Australia. Men who were ousted and remained in Australia, experiencing great sadness and sense of loss.

They have lost their place in the family, day to day interactions with their children and wife. And they all worry about the development of their children without their input and care. Most ousted fathers experience bitterness towards their wife, which does not help reconnect their daily family life.

In turn, this behaviour has a great, negative effect on the couple's children. If the man is not there to be the disciplinary adult, children's behaviour is aggressive towards their mother, who quickly gives up trying to shape the children's behaviour. Young men, particularly, suffer from the father not being in the home. As well as disrespecting their mothers verbally, some youths go out into the streets and become involved in illegal activities. They can cause vandalism, car thefts, shop lifting, rubbish burning. Some deliberately go to a shop such as Big W and steal some small things and are quite relaxed about being arrested. It is asking-for-help behaviour and so far, neither mothers nor fathers in any numbers have taken up the challenge to learn about Parenting in Australia, despite at least one Social worker, attempting to run classes for the mothers in Victoria. Children are used to some physical correction, but they too have discovered that this behaviour is not allowed in Australia. They also know that teachers, police and other significant adults are not allowed to hit them or even shout at them. This is the total opposite of how youths can be treated in South Sudan. Corporal punishment is against the law in Australia, so other ways need to be learned and used by parents and guardians.

A couple of years ago, a group of mothers and a few fathers went to talk with the young men, out in the suburban train stations. This was a new initiative and worked for a number of the youths. Unfortunately, parents gave up, were tired, busy and needed to be at home with their other children. The main problem was the parents lacked training in parenting skills. These skills would have taught them how to verbally, effectively communicate with the youths.

Education about positive parenting is still a major need, for all families. Even families with two parents. Because children are growing up in a new country, facing totally new situations, parents need to learn how to communicate with their children using new skills.

A Focus group of single fathers, recorded the following comments about this situation: Men have the feeling that

> "mothers no longer give the youths all the care they need"
> "Mothers only think of themselves"
> "Fathers should be allowed to visit the children".

Some fathers say they want to be available for their children, but they don't want to live with their former wives. (Gardiner, 2017).

Clearly, this is a major issue and challenge for service providers, while parents need education about Australian Family Law and implementation of parent education training. Men would like to receive this type of training, plus financial management training, according to the Focus Group. Fathers do not get the chance to learn and then implement their learning of new communication skills. (Gardiner, 2017) Women appear to mainly want children to behave without the mother's input. This lack of setting boundaries is not helping children grow up with a sense of right and wrong. It is a serious lapse of taking responsibility by some of the mothers.

Schools comment that they sometimes have a difficult experience with South Sudanese mothers after the mothers are called to school about a child's behaviour. Mothers find it difficult to accept that their child is misbehaving, and they say it is up to the school to teach the children acceptable behaviour. (Gardiner, 2017)

## Legal issues

Men and women need knowledge about Australia's Family Law, to give them understanding of why Australian family law changed in the 1970s. There is great suspicion about all aspects of marriage breakdown and the Child Protection Unit of social work in Australia. Parents believe that the Child Protection Unit genuinely harms the child(ren) and has no right to remove or interact with families.

Parents need to understand about training young people to learn how to live a good life, like driving a car legally. It is hard to understand why parents show little interest in learning new skills. Part of it is to do with the way South Sudanese people learn. Their primary learning comes from looking at other South Sudanese families. They, as has been said earlier, learn from each other about almost everything. Plus they have almost all learnt the same methods of educating and disciplining children which cannot be used in Australia. They need alternatives.

## Cultural

Almost everything cultural was practiced and learnt by the current group of adults and parents. Their culture is very complex. As Lewis Anei Madut-Kuendit says in his book "The Dinka History", South Sudanese are one group with millions of members. Because the culture was oral, instructions on everything were learnt from each other. And, as we all know, to make new changes to a rule, it takes a major reason to bring in a change. For traditional South Sudanese, there has been no such need for change in South Sudan. But in a western country, which has rules against anyone using physical violence for any reason, such as disciplining children, there is now a great need to replace violence with knowledge and parenting skills.

The role of men and women in Australian society needs to be explored and training undertaken by social service organisations to teach men and women about the Laws of Australia.

The concept of women living by "African time" needs to be challenged. There is no need for women being late and women need to understand it is impolite behaviour on their part, to be late for appointments. Being late is actually taken very seriously in Australia because it shows disrespect for the person expecting the woman. It is like they are saying with this behaviour, that they do not have to follow the rules.

Women need to understand what is legally allowed regarding financial management, so that they learn that children receive Centrelink money to provide the children with shoes, clothes and school-based items. It is not supposed to be used for the parent's direct benefit, such as providing money for parties and special clothing.

Single mothers and fathers also need to be taught Positive Parenting skills.

## Education Issues

Firstly, women, men and children needed to learn English – speaking, reading and writing. This is very hard, especially for the older ones.

Single and still married parents need to understand how they can help their children learn better, by setting up quiet places where homework and other schoolwork can be done.

Making nutritious snacks and lunches is important. Correct footwear is important for children.

There could be specific clothing for Sports programs, provided by families.

If a mother's level of skill in English are low, programs to offer further education could be developed, using South Sudanese trainers or teachers.

Many South Sudanese are successful at learning, and many now have tertiary qualifications and employment. Those who came to Australia early in the 1990s, are perhaps the most successful groups of all. This should be a positive proof that given time, everyone will eventually learn the difficult English language.

## Health issues

There are so many reasons for South Sudanese refugees to have some mental health issues. There is very little understanding of what causes mental illness in the cohort.

Traditionally, if a person starts behaving strangely, the person is cared for by the family. But there are no psychiatrists and only a few psychologists in South Sudan for millions of people, with nowhere to take the person for treatment. Some families tie the mentally ill person to a tree, where he/she can receive food and water and be kept in an area where the village can see them. And there is shade. Even the mention of mental health raises anxiety among South Sudanese Australians. This could be part of a healthy living short course, to demonstrate how people can be helped by Counselling and skill development.

During one of the wars, the country's leader, Dr. John Garang wanted to save the lives of youths. He told everyone to send the youths to Ethiopia and Kenya. It took thousands of youths many months to walk so far and hundreds died on the long journey. There were no adults or food or water, boys ate grass, leaves, flowers. Some died because of what they ate and many were taken by wild animals. Thousands of young boys and some girls walking north. They called themselves the Lost Boys. Thousands walked and came to Ethiopia where that government gave them tents, clothing, food, water and education. This experience has stayed in the minds of those boys and some girls and still today, those who are aged in their 40s, have nightmares. They are not treated for mental illness, due to the grave suspicions they hold of mental illness.

Elders need to understand how to stay healthy in Australia. This information could be given in a series of classes or some Elders could be taught the information and could instruct the others.

South Sudanese people consider 45/50 to be old, which stops some women and men from continuing in education. They still expect that their families will take care of them, feed them and take them to their doctor appointments. This has been the case for some Elders, but not all. The tradition of putting one older teenage youth to stay in the Elders home and keep them company is being followed.

All South Sudanese people have come to Australia from war. Years of war without lasting peace. This has had a terrible effect on everyone's mental health. The mental health of men has been further damaged by the failure of their marriages. They feel lost and uncertain about their futures.

All South Sudanese have lost relatives and friends in all the wars and tribal fighting. Grief Counselling would be helpful.

Men were taken to be child soldiers and have PTSD flashbacks.

Many women were raped and some tortured. On one occasion, the President said the Government had insufficient money to pay its soldiers, so a message went out that men could rape any women they wanted to instead of pay.

## Nutrition

Parents should be taught about the importance of good nutrition for themselves and their family.

Men and women are putting on weight and the teeth of little children is very poor, with teeth rotting due to a bad diet.

Past bad experiences with water makes some parents buy sweet fizzy drinks for their children and even fruit juice is full of sugar. Water in

Australia is good for everyone. Eating 3 times a day is new.

In recognition of this lack of knowledge, Africa World Books Community Education will be running a program called "Families Dancing for Health" in Perth, Western Australia in 2020. The aim is to attract South Sudanese families to meet weekly over a 7-week timeline. The first hour will be spent by the families deciding which of their favourite dances could be held.

The next step of three quarters of an hour, is where they are served nutritious snacks made by a Dietician's service called Ishar. Ishar is a multi-cultural women's health service and AWBCE is proud to have this service as a partner in education. Recipes will be given, and the adults will be offered a further 4 opportunities to learn about Nutrition and what foods help grow the children best.

The final hour will be to practice the dance and any other dance that they want. At week 7, there will be a celebration where the food is nutritious, and some traditional food is served. The aim is to change meal choices being made by the families or mothers. And the dancing is a very healthy form of exercise.

After the 7 weeks, a 4-week cooking course will be offered, so that recipes can be tried.

## Children and Youths

Parent education training courses give knowledge and skill development and are much needed.

Children do well at schools and are friendly and helpful. Parents play an important role in their children's education.

Parents have responsibilities to their children to provide any uniform, nutritious lunches and a safe quiet place for doing homework.

Children and youths become used to school and sporting games more quickly than their parents adapt.

## Areas of conflict

There are changes in the roles of men and women in Australia. People need to learn about the differences and gain some relevant communication skills.

Parents can fight with their children over many issues. It is wise for the parent to first listen to their child and then decide whose responsibility the issue is.

Parents must learn to make rules in their family, that they can keep. Design them with the input of children and teenagers. This is good because children and adults learn and it teaches children that they have responsibilities too: not just the parents. In Australia a family is like a team, with everyone doing good things for the family.

## The Future

The main suggestion is around education. There is so much to learn about life in a western country. People find adapting to the new country to be hard. All the former refugees say they are happy to be in Australia. They love the peace, food, freedom to say what they think, places to visit, a car to drive, doctors to see when needed. Many South Sudanese Australians attend education and add to their existing qualifications.

Most former refugees become Australian citizens and participate in voting with great joy.

Young people are doing well at school, despite the state of disarray that their parents are in. Many children have been badly affected by their parent's experiences, young people are making their own way academically and they are very good at Sport.

Life can only improve for the former refugees. They enjoy learning, so their futures will be bright.

REFERENCES
Abur, W and Spaaij R, 2016. "Settlement and employment experiences of South Sudanese people from refugee backgrounds in Melbourne, Australia". Australasian Review of African Studies, Vol 37, Number 2, December 2016
Gardiner, E, 2017. "Investigating Culture Related Settlement Challenges among the Dinka Community in Melbourne" Masters Thesis, Victoria University.
Madut-Kuendit, LA 2016, The Dinka History, Perth, Africa World Books. The Sudanese Tribune, 2017.

Sudan

*Khartoum and the River Nile*

# Sudan

## Sudan and Wars

One of the most common characteristics of Sudan is the number of wars and border disputes Sudan has waged and keeps waging. It has fights going on in several areas of its borders, in particular. And yet it also is able to farm and export certain goods overseas.

There have been 2 Civil wars – 1955 – 1972 and 1983 – 2005, plus there is still skirmishing and fighting in Darfur and Abyai. Sudan has a history of aggression which is greater than that for surrounding countries.

Sudan is an African country in the East part of the Horn of Africa group. Other countries are Eritrea, Ethiopia, Djibouti, Somalia and South Sudan. All six countries share some aspects of life, such as Terrain, Religion, Tribal life and even some parts of their Cultures. Sudan is surrounded by South

Sudan, Central African Republic, Chad, Libya, Egypt, Eritrea and Ethiopia and has some coastline along the Red Sea with a Port, the Port of Sudan. There are some still disputed areas of Darfur and Abyei, with which Sudan has waged a constant war for years.

Sudan is a mainly Islamic country and according to many writers, the religion is a more significant characteristic than their indigenous tribes. Sudan and South Sudan were each part of a single country, Sudan, until a Referendum gave South Sudan the opportunity to become a separate country in its own right. South Sudan is the world's newest country and chose that outcome in 2011 when 98.8% of the South Sudanese population chose to become independent.

## Britain and Sudan

Britain has been active with Sudan for around 200 years, as a ruling body. Sudan is an Arabic, Islamic country with a population of over 40 million people. It has 18 States, although North Darfur, South, East, Central and West Darfur want to be separate from Sudan. Sudan is also accused of using genocide against South Sudan during the long war leading to South Sudan becoming a separate country in 2011. Omar Bashir was the person ultimately responsible. Lt. Gen. Omar Hassan Ahmad al-Bashir.

The name Sudan is an Arabic expression - bilad al-sudan ("land of the blacks"). Medieval Arab geographers referred to African countries that began at the southern edge of the Sahara Desert. The Islamic religion and Arabic as a language became most characteristic of the northern countries of Africa and the Black Africans with older languages and cultures were more in the south. (Britannica 2019)

Britain invaded and occupied Egypt in 1882 to quell a nationalist revolution. They wanted to oppose foreign powers, such as France. Any occupying power needed to rule the Nile River areas by clearing away any foreign powers. The British were able to negotiate peace agreements

*Sudan*

SCENE 3° WAR IN THE SOUDAN, WITH TERRIFIC ENCOUNTERS, ASSAULTS, NAVAL COMBATS & WARLIKE EPISODES.

with Italy and Germany to have them stay out of Sudan. French forces wanted Britain out of Egypt.

In 1897 British forces realized that they must capture Sudan and keep the French out. Lord Kitchener invaded Sudan. He defeated a large Mahdist army in 1898. Kitchener had 20,000 and the Mahdist army was 60,000. It took only a half day on September 2 to defeat the opposition.

An Anglo-French agreement was signed in 1899. It said French expansion east would stop at the Nile. Sudan was given separate political status. But still there were local skirmishes among Southerners and a couple of foreign powers. Britain took the lead and kept religious uprisings suppressed. Civil administrators gradually replaced the army. The South was also under British rule, but never to be fully subdued. The British were not able to rule as closely as they had in other countries.

In 1924, the Governor General was assassinated. The British killed most of the soldiers and British rule continued. In 1943 the first real political party was formed. They were militants. The moderates wanted to cooperate with Britain towards independence. But the political parties hated each other and this "strangled" parliamentary government.

These groups controlled Sudanese politics until the 1990s. In 1947 Britain began southern participation in the Legislative Council.

British rule changed in 1951 the earlier Treaty of 1936 continued, and they proclaimed Egyptian rule over the Sudan. That continued the troubles with the South, until after two civil wars, the South chose in a Referendum, to become an independent country in 2011. Both countries still clash at times over border issues, ownership of large oil stocks, plus tribal clashes.

For the next 30 and more years, groups in the north became increasingly nationalist and violent. Agreements were made with many groups, but peace was always broken. During this period, the South began to get organized and started to organize so that a new government structure began for the South. One of the civil wars lasted for 20 years and was bitterly fought, until A Comprehensive Peace Agreement was signed in 2005. The CPA in turn led to the South gaining its full independence from the North in 2011.

The past 120 - 150 years have been filled with violence, battles, broken agreements. In Melbourne there are many former citizens of both the South and the North.

*A Map showing the North and South Sudan countries.*

Khartoum
University

# Khartoum

Sudan's capital, Khartoum, is located roughly in the centre of the country, at the junction of the Blue Nile and White Nile rivers. These tributaries of the Nile, link Ethiopia and South Sudan to Sudan. It is part of the largest urban area in Sudan and is a centre of commerce as well as of government. Sudan inherited its boundaries from Anglo-Egyptian Sudan, established in 1899.

Khartoum, the capital city, has approximately 4.632 million people. The largest cities are Omdurman, 2,395,159; Port Sudan, 489,275 and the monetary unit is the Dinar. The languages are mainly Arabic (official), English (official), Nubian, Ta Bedawie, Fur. And the predominant ethnicity/race is Sudanese Arab (approximately 70%), Fur, Beja, Nuba, Fallata. The largest religion is Sunni Muslim with a small Christian minority. The literacy rate is 71.9% (2011 estimated). Since the secession of South Sudan in July 2011, estimates place the current population of Sudan at about 42 million.

## Industries

Income per capita is $2,600. Inflation sits at 25%. Unemployment is 20% (2012 estimated). Arable land is small, 6.76%. Agriculture consists of cotton, groundnuts (peanuts), sorghum, millet, wheat, gum arabic, sugarcane, cassava (tapioca), mangos, papaya, bananas, sweet potatoes, sesame; sheep, livestock. The labor force is 11.92 million (2007 est.); agriculture employs 80% of the workforce, industry employs 7%, and services employ 13% (1998 est.).

Sudan's Industries are oil, cotton ginning, textiles, cement, edible oils, sugar, soap distilling, shoes, petroleum refining, pharmaceuticals, armaments, automobile/light truck assembly. Its natural resources are petroleum; small reserves of iron ore, copper, chromium ore, zinc, tungsten, mica, silver, gold, hydropower. Exports: $4.145 billion (2013 est.): gold; oil and petroleum products; cotton, sesame, livestock, groundnuts, gum arabic, sugar. Sudan imports $5.941 billion (2013 est) and foodstuffs, manufactured goods, refinery and transport equipment, medicines and chemicals, textiles, wheat.

## War and border disputes

One of the largest issues for Sudan come from the several wars and border disputes Sudan is waging with other countries. International disputes: the effects of Sudan's almost constant ethnic and rebel militia fighting since the mid-20th century have penetrated all of the neighboring states; Chad wishes to be a helpful mediator in resolving the Darfur conflict, and in 2010 established a joint border monitoring force with Sudan, which has helped to reduce cross-border banditry and violence; as of mid-2013, Chad, Egypt, Ethiopia, Israel, the Central African Republic, and South Sudan provided shelter for more than 600,000 Sudanese refugees; during the same period, Sudan, in turn, hosted about 115,000 Eritreans, 32,000

Chadians, and smaller numbers of Ethiopians and Central Africans; Sudan accuses Eritrea of supporting Sudanese rebel groups; efforts to demarcate the porous boundary with Ethiopia proceed slowly due to civil and ethnic fighting in eastern Sudan; Sudan claims but Egypt de facto administers security and economic development of the Halaib region north of the 22nd parallel boundary; periodic violent skirmishes with Sudanese residents over water and grazing rights persist among related pastoral populations along the border with the Central African Republic; South Sudan-Sudan boundary represents 1 January 1956 alignment, with the final alignment pending negotiations and demarcation; final sovereignty status of Abyei Area pending negotiations between South Sudan and Sudan. One other issue involving violent interactions is the major deposits of oil half of which was given to South Sudan in 2005. Sudan wants all of the oil and South Sudan cannot afford to build a parallel pipe to Port Sudan and there is no guarantee that Sudan would welcome this in any case.

Diplomacy has so far failed to achieve positive outcomes for any and all of these war-like situations.

> "Ever since Lt. Gen. Omar Bashir's military coup in 1989, the de facto ruler of Sudan had been Hassan el-Turabi, a cleric and political leader who is a major figure in the pan-Arabic Islamic fundamentalist resurgence. In 1999, however, Bashir ousted Turabi and placed him under house arrest. (He was freed in Oct. 2003.) Since then Bashir has made overtures to the West, and in Sept. 2001, the UN lifted its six-year-old sanctions. The U.S., however, still officially considers Sudan a terrorist state.
>
> A cease-fire was declared between the Sudanese government and the Sudan People's Liberation Army (SPLA) in July 2002. During peace talks, which continued through 2003, the government agreed to a power-sharing government for six years, to be followed by a referendum on self-determination for the south. Fighting on both sides continued throughout the peace negotiations". (Infoplease.com 2019)

Since 1999 international attention has been focused on evidence that slavery is widespread throughout Sudan. Arab raiders from the north of the country have enslaved thousands of southerners, who are black. The Dinka people have been the hardest-hit. Some sources point out that the raids intensified in the 1980s along with the civil war between north and south.

The 4 regions of Darfur have been locked in conflict with Sudan which lays claim to this whole region. Arab – north Sudan militias, believed to have been armed by the government, have killed between 200,000 and 300,000 civilians and displaced more than 1 million. While the war in the south was fought against black Christians and animists, the Darfur conflict is being fought against black Muslims. Although the international community has reacted with alarm to the humanitarian disaster—unmistakably the world's worst—it has been ineffective in persuading the Sudanese government to rein in the Janjaweed. Janjaweed are armed soldiers who carry out raids and kidnaps of opposition mostly civilians. Despite the European Union and the United States describing the killing as genocide, and despite a UN Security Council resolution demanding that Sudan stop the Arab militias, the killing continued throughout 2005. Helicopter gunships were even used on traditional villages. (Info please)

In 2006, the slaughter in Darfur escalated, and the Khartoum government remained defiantly indifferent to the international communities' calls to stop the violence. The 7,000 African Union (AU) peacekeepers deployed to Darfur proved too small and ill equipped a force to prevent much of it. A fragile peace deal in May 2006 was signed between the Sudanese government and the main Darfur rebel group.

In July 2007, the UN Security Council voted unanimously to deploy as many as 26,000 peacekeepers from the African Union and the United Nations forces to help end the violence in Darfur. The African Union peacekeeper base in Darfur was attacked in September. Ten peacekeepers were killed. Days later, the town was razed, leaving some 7,000 Darfuris homeless (Wikipedia 2019).

The Sudanese government refused to hand over them over to the International Criminal Court. Kushayb, a Janjuween leader, was arrested by Sudanese police in October 2008. He was not, however, handed over to the ICC.

The Bush administration expanded sanctions on Sudan in May, banning 31 Sudanese companies and four individuals from doing business in the U.S.

After some years of relative calm following the 2005 agreement which ended the second Sudanese civil war between the Sudanese government and SPLM rebels, fighting broke out again in the lead-up to South Sudan independence on 9 July 2011, starting in South Kordofan on 5 June and spreading to the neighboring Blue Nile state in September. SPLM-N, splitting from newly-independent SPLM, took up arms against the inclusion of the two southern states in Sudan with no popular consultation and against the lack of democratic elections.

As of October 2014, some two million people have been affected by the conflict, with more than 500,000 having been displaced and about 250,000 of them fleeing to South Sudan and Ethiopia. In January 2015, fighting intensified as Omar al-Bashir's government tried to regain control of rebel-held territory ahead of April 2015 general elections.

With the overthrow of al-Bashir in April 2019 following months of protests, the SRF announced a three-month ceasefire, hoping to facilitate a Sudanese transition to democracy. This led to the beginning of peace negotiations between the rebels and the new interim government. The Sudanese peace process was formalised with the August 2019 Draft Constitutional Declaration, signed by military and civilian representatives during the Sudanese Revolution, that mandates that a peace agreement be made in South Kordofan and Blue Nile (and in Darfur) within the first six months of the 39-month transition period to democratic civilian government.

"Since 1983, Muslims in the north have been fighting a jihad against non-muslims in the south". (Tibi, B., 2008 Political Islam, World Politics and Europe, Routledge p33)

## Demographics

Sudan has 597 groups that speak over 400 different languages and dialects. [218] Sudanese Arabs are by far the largest ethnic group in Sudan. They are almost entirely Muslims.

The majority of Arabised and indigenous tribes like the Fur, Zaghawa, Borgo, Masalit and some Baggara ethnic groups, who speak Chadian Arabic, show less cultural integration because of cultural, linguistic and genealogical variations with other Arab and Arabised tribes.

## Beja nomads

The vast majority of Arab tribes in Sudan migrated into the Sudan in the 12th century, intermarried with the indigenous Nubian and other African populations and introduced Islam.

Sudan consists of numerous other non-Arabic groups, such as the Masalit, Zaghawa, Fulani, Northern Nubians, Nuba, and the Beja people.

There is also a small, but prominent Greek community.

Approximately 70 languages are native to Sudan. Sudanese Arabic is the most widely spoken language in the country. the country has been influenced by Nilotic, Arab, and western cultures. Few nomads in Sudan still have similar accents to the ones in Saudi Arabia. As with South Sudan, a number of Nilo-Saharan languages are also spoken in Sudan. Fur speakers inhabit the west (Darfur), with perhaps a million speakers. There are likewise various Nubian languages, with over 6 million speakers along the Nile in the north. The most linguistically diverse region in the country is the Nuba Hills area in Kordofan, inhabited by speakers of multiple language families,

# Religion

"At the 2011 division which split off South Sudan, over 97% of the population in the remaining Sudan adheres to Islam" (Wikipedia, 2019).

Long-established groups of Coptic Orthodox and Greek Orthodox Christians exist in Khartoum and other northern cities. Ethiopian and Eritrean Orthodox communities also exist in Khartoum and eastern Sudan, largely made up of refugees and migrants from the past few decades. The Sudan Evangelical Presbyterian Church also has membership.

Almost everyone from the north of Sudan is a Muslim. That means there are certain behaviours which Muslims observe. They must pray 5 times a day, they must observe a month of fasting – Ramadan.

In Australia, there is a range of activities and ways of living. There is choice in the Muslim religion, just as there is for Christianity and once you

*A Sufi Dervish ready to worship on Friday afternoon*

get to know a Muslim or a family, you can see that even in families, people make choices about dress and other matters. Muslims have Sharia law, which is broadly applied to the daily life of Muslims.

Sharia Law in Arabic means "the way," and does not refer to a body of law. Sharia is more accurately understood as referring to wide-ranging moral and broad ethical principles drawn from the Quran and the practices and sayings (hadith) of Prophet Muhammad.

Sharia is believed by Muslims to be the divinely ordained legal system of Islam. It governs every aspect of life: politics, economics, hygiene, marriage and family relationships, diet, warfare, crime. Everything is covered.

There are major celebrations – Muharram – Islamic New Year

Mawlid al Nabi – Prophet Mohammed's birthday

Eid al-Fitr – Conclusion of Ramadan

Eid al-Adha – Celebration concluding the Hajj

Major holidays – Ramadan – Each year in the 9th month

Laylat al-Qadr – The Night of Power

Hajj – Each year in the 12th month

You can wish a Muslim happy Ramadan – *Ramadan Kareem* or *Ramadan Mubarak.*

Some Muslim men do not like to shake hands with a woman, so wait until you see what a Muslim man indicates.

If you do shake someone's hand, it is just like placing your hand gently, not squeezed as firmly a Caucasian Australian might do.

Because a Muslim man is head of the family, he could expect you to address him first.

It is a woman's choice to wear or not, a hijab or shawl for the head.

*Sudan*

# Religion and health issues
From: www.islam-usa.com/e40.html

- Cleanliness is considered "half of the faith". Qur'an, the holy book, prohibits eating pork or pork products, meat of dead animals, blood and all intoxicants.
- Respect a Muslim's modesty and privacy. Some health examinations can be done over a gown. Provide same sex health care persons, if possible. Always examine a female patient in the presence of another female.
- Some Muslim men will not shake a woman's hand.
- Provide Muslim or Kosher meals.
- Allow them to pray, and if they can read, to read the Qur'an.
- Take time to explain medical tests, procedures and treatment.
- During a birthing, it is preferred that the father be the sole male present.

There is also a range of deep cultural beliefs and attitudes in Muslim communities towards disability that need to be discussed. They are:
- A social stigma with corresponding fear of "visibility" in the community.
- A curse or punishment for some wrongdoing. This belief is evident among other cultures.
- A gift from God or God-given, when a disadvantaged child or person is seen as a blessing.

## Christian and Muslim families

Family is the foundation of Sudanese society. The peace and security offered by a stable family unit is greatly valued and is seen as essential for the spiritual growth of its members. A harmonious social order is created by the existence of extended families. Children are treasured, and rarely leave home until they marry.

## Christians, Muslims and the Elderly

In Sudan, there are no old peoples' homes. The practice of caring for one's elderly relatives is considered an honour and blessing, and an opportunity for great spiritual growth. God asks that we pray for our parents, but act with limitless compassion, remembering that when we were helpless little children, they preferred to help us rather than themselves.

Mothers are particularly respected in both religions. The Prophet Mohammed said "Paradise lies at the feet of mothers".

When they reach old age, Sudanese parents are treated mercifully, with kindness and selflessness. Serving one's parents is a duty second only to prayer, and it is their right to expect it. It is considered despicable to express any irritation, if an old person becomes difficult.

Respite care and nursing homes may be used. Hospitals are also acceptable to many, however people without English are frightened about remaining in mainstream institutions.

## Communication of diagnosis/prognosis in a medical situation

News of an illness is first given to the family – the closest member to the patient. The next of kin will advise the immediate family, but perhaps advice will not be given to friends.

Patients are often not told about a life-threatening disease, as it is felt that to do so might make their condition worse. They also may be ostracized by their community because people may consider them infectious and/or cursed.

Every family is different. Plus, after being in a western country for several years, the understanding of English could be fairly good, so it might be possible to tell the person gently about the diagnosis. If a patient wants to know, tell him/her.

In some cases, the family leaves all the telling to the medical staff, in other families, the wisest person will manage the telling.

Words like "dying" and "cancer" are used with sensitivity, as for any group. Cancer is sometimes referred to as "That Disease". Avoid discussing death, dying and how long a person is likely to live.

When a person is dying, family and friends are called in to stay until the person passes away. The Qur'an is recited until they pass away. Once the person has died, the house is open, and condolences are received. There are no celebrations or frivolities. Burial and religious rites are performed within 24 hours.

## Music

Music has a large number of iterations and has suffered government intrusions as instruments and performers were said to be doing something forbidden to Islam. Interestingly, European instruments were used, and the Scottish bagpipes were popular and used in playing new music. Northern areas of Sudan are called Aidlayib which is played on a Tambur, a five stringed wooden instrument.

## Photography

The use of photography in Sudan goes back to the 1880s and the Anglo-Egyptian rule As in other countries, the growing importance of photography for mass media like newspapers, as well as for amateur photographers led to a wider photographic documentation and use of photographs in Sudan during the 20th century and beyond.

## Education

Education in Sudan is free and compulsory for children aged 6 to 13 years, although more than 40% of children are not going to schools due to the economic situation. Environmental and social factors also increase the difficulty of getting to school, especially for girls.[230] Primary education consists of eight years, followed by three years of secondary education. The former educational ladder 6 + 3 + 3 was changed in 1990. The primary language at all levels is Arabic. Schools are concentrated in urban areas; many in the west have been damaged or destroyed by years of civil war. In 2001 the World Bank estimated that primary enrollment was 46 percent of eligible pupils and 21 percent of secondary students. Enrollment varies widely, falling below 20 percent in some provinces. The literacy rate is 70.2% of total population, male 79.6%, female 60.8%. There is a bias towards boys receiving education rather than girls.

## Health and Population

Sudan has a life expectancy of 65.1 years according to the latest data for the year 2019 from the macrotrends. Infant mortality in 2016 was 44.8 per 1,000.

UNICEF estimates that 87% of Sudanese women and girls between the ages of 15 to 49 have had female genital mutilation performed on them.

0-14 years: 43.07% (male 9,434,634 /female 9,136,951)
15-24 years: 20.22% (male 4,459,335 /female 4,259,341)
25-54 years: 29.8% (male 6,236,954 /female 6,612,593)
55-64 years: 3.93% (male 876,614 /female 819,048)
65 years and over: 2.98% (male 688,391 /female 596,982) (2018 est.)

## Water Politics

The Nile River is the longest in the world while the Nile Basin covers 1.3 million square miles, making it slightly larger than India. There are ten riparian countries Egypt, Sudan, Ethiopia, Uganda, Tanzania, Kenya, Democratic Republic of the Congo, Rwanda, Burundi, and Eritrea. Three of the ten Egypt, Sudan and Ethiopia are far more important than the remaining seven from the standpoint of Nile water hydrology and potential political conflict or cooperation.

## The United States of America

The United States played a key role in helping negotiate the 2005 Comprehensive Peace Agreement (CPA), 2005, between Sudan and Sudan Peoples' Liberation Movement (SPLM) that laid the groundwork for South Sudan's 2011 independence referendum and secession. Several disputes between Sudan and South Sudan remain unresolved post-independence, including border demarcation and the status of the Abyei region. The United States supports the efforts of the African Union (AU) to help the countries work through these issues.

Another issue unresolved by the CPA was the status within Sudan of Southern Kordofan and Blue Nile states – the "Two Areas." In mid-2011, following South Sudan's independence, conflict broke out between the government and the SPLM-N in the Two Areas, effectively suspending the "popular consultations" called for in the CPA The SPLM-N and the Government of Sudan have not resolved the conflict in the Two Areas. The ongoing conflict has severely affected or displaced more than 1.1 million people within the Two Areas and caused more than 300,000 people to flee to neighboring countries.

In 2003, non-Arabs in the western region of Darfur, who since 1990 have accused the government of systematic discrimination, marginalization, and oppression, rebelled against the government, protesting decades of political and economic neglect. The government responded with brutal force, including the use of Arab militias known as Janjaweed. In the ensuing conflict, more than 300,000 people were killed. To date, the conflict in Darfur has affected 4.7 million people, including more than 1.76 million internally displaced persons (IDPs) in need of humanitarian assistance.

Since 1987," As the largest international donor of humanitarian aid in Sudan, the United States continues to provide impartial, needs-based assistance to all accessible areas and populations, including displaced and otherwise conflict-affected people, individuals living in camp for IDPs, local communities hosting IDPs, and formerly displaced returnees. The United States supports democratic development in Sudan, as well as a transition from emergency assistance to development assistance where conditions and security allow" (US Bureau of African Affairs, 2019)

*Sudan*

# Role and acceptable behaviours of health professionals/volunteers

It would be preferable if the treating professionals are the same gender as the patient. Some men will not shake hands with a woman.

Many families remove their shoes at the door.

Visitors to a Muslim home should be aware that alcoholic drinks are not permitted. Pig in any form is forbidden. Meat must be Halal – slaughtered in a special way with prayers being said.

Health professionals should be aware that Muslims wash and then pray five times a day.

All pain relief is allowed.

Information provision is helpful, and the language of the family members must be considered. Many refugees speak 4 or sometimes more, languages and English may not be their main language.

Other ways of sharing information is to call a meeting, run a forum, hold a discussion seminar, use the language of the people being worked with.

REFERENCES
https://www.bing.com/images/search?q=Activities+in+Sudan&FORM=RESTAB
https://www.bing.com/search?q=muslim+sharia+law+australia&form=EDGEAR&qs=AS&cvid=541e63bb86b6476da8e69d928c13f0c2&cc=US&setlang=en-US&plvar=0&PC=ASTS
https://www.bing.com/search?q=US%20Bureau%20of%20African%20Affairs&qs=n&form=QBRE&sp=-1&ghc=1&pq=us%20bureau%20of%20african%20affairs&sc=2-28&sk=&cvid=D388530BB80543B896C11B1CA0563249
https://www.bing.com/search?q=Wikipedia&qs=n&form=QBRE&sp=-1&pq=wikipedia&sc=8-9&sk=&cvid=A809DC55563846B999F72CA0D3D313D5
https://www.britannica.com/place/Sudan/The-British-conquest
https://www.cia.gov/library/publications/the-world-factbook/geos/su.html
htps://www.infoplease.com/world/countries/sudan/history
https://www.state.gov/u-s-relations-with-sudan/
Tibi, B., 2008 Political Islam, World Politics and Europe, Routledge, p33.

## A Note from the Publisher

The publisher wishes to acknowledge and thank Dr Douglas H. Johnson for his invaluable help and support for Africa World Books and its mission of preserving and promoting African cultural and literary traditions and history. Dr Johnson and fellow historians have been instrumental in ensuring that African people remain connected to their past and their identity. Africa World Books is proud to carry on this mission.

www.ingramcontent.com/pod-product-compliance
Lightning Source LLC
Chambersburg PA
CBHW020325010526
44107CB00054B/1979